SEEDS
OF
SUCCESS

BY

JOY HANEY

Seeds of Success
by Joy Haney

© 2009

Cover design by Laura Jurek

Printed in the United States of America

ISBN# 978-1-880969-58-8

Author's disclaimer: This book contains material collected for many years. Since starting this manuscript I have done my best in working with the library and Internet resources to document the source of each quote. Some could not be found, and memory is vague concerning the books, read so many years ago, where these quotes were found. Enjoy the nuggets of truth, and pass them to a friend and your children. Do not let these ideas die.

TABLE OF CONTENTS

CHAPTERS:
SEEDS OF SUCCESS:

The greatest achievement of the human spirit is to live up to one's opportunities and make the most of one's resources.
— VAUVENARGUES

The willingness to take risks is our grasp of faith.
— GEORGE E. WOODBERRY

What is defeat? Nothing but education, nothing but the first step to something better.
— WENDELL PHILLIPS

A happy person is not a person in a certain set of circumstances, but rather a person with a certain set of attitudes.
— HUGH DOWNS

What we do on some great occasion will probably depend on what we already are; and what we are will be the result of previous years of self-discipline.
                                        —H.P. LIDDON

They can conquer who believe they can.
                                        —VIRGIL

The real difference between men is energy. A strong will, a settled purpose, an invincible determination, can accomplish almost anything; and in this lies the distinction between great men and little men.
                                        —THOMAS FULLER

Not he who has much is rich, but he who gives much.
                                        —ERICH FROMM

The improvement of understanding is for two ends: first, our own increase of knowledge; secondly, to enable us to deliver that knowledge to others.
                                        —JOHN LOCKE

Prayer is an invitation to God to intervene in our lives.
                                        —ABRAHAM JOSHUA HESCHEL

Books won't stay banned. They won't burn. Ideas won't go to jail.
                                        —ALFRED WHITNEY GRISWOLD

I have learned that success is to be measured not so much by the position that one has reached in life as by the obstacles which he has overcome while trying to succeed.
— BOOKER T. WASHINGTON

When the best things are not possible, the best may be made of those that are.
— RICHARD HOOKER

It is not what he has, nor even what he does, which directly affects the worth of a man; but what he is.
— HENRI-FREDERIC AMIEL

The worst bankrupt in the world is the man who has lost his enthusiasm.
— H. W. ARNOLD

Keep away from people who try to belittle your ambitions. Small people always do that, but the really great make you feel that you, too, can become great.
— MARK TWAIN

The heights by great men reached and kept
Were not attained by sudden flight,
But they, while their companions slept
Were toiling upward in the night.
— HENRY W. LONGFELLOW

Great souls have wills; feeble ones have only wishes.
— CHINESE PROVERB

It is one of the most beautiful compensations of this life that no man can sincerely try to help another without helping himself.
— RALPH WALDO EMERSON

When you get into a tight place and everything goes against you, till it seems as though you could not hold on a minute longer, never give up then, for that is just the place and time that the tide will turn.
— HARRIET BEECHER STOWE

ACKNOWLEDGEMENTS

A book is born in the mind of an individual and bursts forth into fruition with much hard work, and with others helping along the way. This is to acknowledge those who helped make this book happen.

Honor and respect and eternal thanksgiving to the Lord Jesus Christ who gave me inspiration and strength to bring forth this book!

Special thanks to my husband, Kenneth Haney, who encourages me to write and allows me to pursue this gift.

Thanks to all the great ones from the past whose works or quotes are included in this book.

Thanks to Kristi LaRiche who works with me on getting the publishing done.

Thanks to Bethany Sledge for her fine help with proof reading.

Thanks to Laura Jurek for her excellent work on the cover design.

Thanks to Gerald Fosdick for his computer design.

Thanks to Larry Craig for all the finishing touches and help.

Thanks to Brian Crain for his great help in formatting the book and creating files for the printer.

Thanks to Reverend Lee Stoneking, a special friend of our family and successful worldwide Evangelist, for writing the blurb for the back of the book.

For all the experiences of life that have taught me what real success is, I give thanks to Jesus for "His candle" that brought light to my mind during the difficult moments of trial.

To you the reader, may the real Author speak to you as you read this collection of "Seeds for Success."

PREFACE

This book has been written to help light a fire in your soul, to lift you up from the doldrums of despair, to infuse you with hope, to let you gaze through the maze of mediocrity into the realm of greatness. May it expand your thinking and influence your behavior into levels of excellence. Whatever you dream of becoming, you can become, whether a better mother, father, educator, doctor, politician, minister, administrator, teacher, writer, scientist, or whatever role you pursue.

You may wonder, "Where is the road to success? How can I feel fulfilled? When will the glow of satisfaction come?" Or you may be ready to quit—throw in the towel—give up on your dream. Maybe life has knocked you down, spun you around until you are dizzy, or left you feeling disappointed and sad? Do you feel like others are "lucky" and that they get all the breaks; are you stewing and fretting about what you want to do but somehow cannot seem to do it? Does it seem that nothing works—everything is a dead-end street, and you find yourself constantly making wrong turns that lead nowhere?

If you are at the end, or even if you know a measure of success, but still experience a realization gnawing at you of not having quite made it, or if you are on your way but are tempted to give up because of the price, this book is for you. It is a practical view of what men and women can do to attain that feeling of fulfillment. This book is filled with success stories of people who made it, often as a result of failing first or of being surrounded by impossibilities.

Dream your dream—do not give up! An unknown author once wrote, "We grow great by dreams. All great people are dreamers. They see things in the soft haze of a spring day or in the red fire of a long winter's evening. Some of us let these great dreams die, but others nourish and protect them, nurse them through bad days 'til they bring them into the sunshine and light that always comes to those who sincerely believe that their dreams will come true."

There will be, as there always have been, crises, wars, troubles, and insurmountable odds to overcome. Each generation has its set of problems, horrors, and difficulties with which to deal. Within the heart of each individual is the power to choose what to do with what life has handed him: to lose or to win! This book is a collection of "seeds of success" from the past to help guide you and shine a light on your pathway. You can make it if you want to bad enough!

Winston Churchill said, "The farther back you can look, the farther forward you are likely to see."

Life is a journey. Many of the "seeds of success" were articulated or written by successful men and women who paved the way before this generation. Their blood, sweat, tears, and determination have left their imprint on each page.

For the people who want to be the best they can be, this book is to help them achieve that goal.

Live today as if you were planting a tomorrow, for what you do today will dictate tomorrow. Just as a garden's harvest is determined by what is planted, so is a life. Someone once said, "Sow an act and you reap a habit; sow a habit and you reap a character; sow a character and you reap a destiny."

The Bible speaks of being successful and prosperous. The following are two of my favorite passages of Scripture on this subject:

Joshua 1:8: "This book of the law shall not depart out of thy mouth; but thou shalt meditate therein day and night, that thou mayest observe to do according to all that is written therein: for then thou shalt make thy way prosperous, and then thou shalt have good success."

Psalm 1:1-3: "Blessed is the man that walketh not in the counsel of the ungodly, nor standeth in the way of sinners, nor sitteth in the seat of the scornful. But his delight is in the law of the LORD; and in his law doth he meditate day and night. And he shall be like a tree planted by the rivers of water, that bringeth forth his fruit in his season; his leaf also shall not wither; and whatsoever he doeth shall prosper."

In each of these instances, both prosperity and success were associated with meditating on the law of God. True success will have its roots in the Bible and the biblical principles found therein, for the Word of God will not return void but will return results, as stated in Isaiah 55:10-11:

"For as the rain cometh down, and the snow from heaven, and returneth not thither, but watereth the earth, and maketh it bring forth and bud, that it may give seed to the sower, and bread to the eater: so shall my word be that goeth forth out of my mouth: it shall not return unto me void, but it shall accomplish that which I please, and it shall prosper in the thing whereto I sent it." The WORD prospers the one who reads it and lives by it!

> *Prosperity does not exalt the wise man, nor does adversity cast him down.*
> —SENECA THE YOUNGER (5? BC-AD 65)

God has given us seeds with which to sow good things. What is a seed? A seed is a grain or ripened ovule of a flowering plant containing an embryo and capable normally of germination to produce a new plant. An embryo is something as yet undeveloped or a beginning of something. Simply said a seed is the beginning of something that will germinate into a new plant. It is up to each individual what is done with those seeds. Some of those seeds or ideas are expanded and talked about in this book. Life is a venture, so live it the best you know how, with help from God's Word, and from those who have walked before you! Let a light go on in the brain, and may you be inspired to live life to the fullest as God meant it to be lived!

Seeds sown today will bloom tomorrow. Nothing happens overnight where seeds are involved. It takes time, but whatever is planted will germinate into something that resembles the seed. So sow well, for you shall reap if you faint not [Galatians 6:9]. Be careful of the seeds you choose to sow! This book will give you 20 seeds that will help you live a successful life in God! Read the book, digest it, practice it and enjoy the results!

DEDICATION

I dedicate this book first to my husband, Kenneth F. Haney, who has been successful and attributes his success to his God.

When I first began this book years ago my first thought was of my children: something to leave with them if God delays the rapture of the Church, and now my grandchildren.

I dedicate this book to my five children, their spouses, and my grandchildren (listed according to birth sequence):

Sherrie Woodward

Nathaniel and Kim Haney

Stephenie and Asbel Montes

Elizabeth and John Shivers

Angela Haney

Mychail Haney

Jonathan Shivers

Kailah Haney

Brittany Shivers

Joshua Haney

Dylan Woodward

Giahna Haney

Aunalee Haney

Dawson Woodward

FOREWORD

With recent tragedies in the past few years, such as the violent massacre on the campus of Virginia Tech and the shootings at the mall that drew national attention, there is an alarming reckoning that a new generation does not hold the same values as the former generation did. I was born in the '40s, and growing up as a child, I played in the streets of the neighborhood without fear of gangs or drive-by shootings. There was a different atmosphere in America than there is today.

I still believe there are millions of people who want the value system that made America great. There is still hope for those who desire to be truly successful and happy. This book is filled with truths from past generations of men and women who were respected in their day as being successful. The same principles that worked then will still work today, for they are timeless, tested, and true.

As an author, I have lived many years and had many experiences. I have seen the good and the bad. Things come and go, and difficult circumstances come to all, rich or poor. It is not always what happens that matters the most but how the person reacts to what happens to him. For me, there have been wonderful times and trying times. There have been valleys to walk through, mountains to climb, and bitter experiences to overcome. There have been joys as well as sorrows, sadness and happiness, good things and bad things, but it has been a wonderful life.

I have learned that to walk in conjunction with the principles set forth in the Book of all books is as important as breathing. To have to stumble through life without knowing how or where to go is tragic, but to know the way, because of God's guidance and lessons learned from successful fellow travelers, is fulfilling.

Each of the following subjects is important and will help you to achieve the success in life that you so desire, for to have the hands full, but to feel empty inside is dreadful. To be able to sleep at night feeling inner peace is incredible. To feel the glow of having done something to help another is priceless. There is a way to live that brings true success and God's favor, and you will find it in this book!

This book has been a work in progress, as it was started over fifteen years ago. I worked on it, put it away, worked at it some more and put it away, but now is the time for it to be published. God has helped me with the many challenges it has presented. May you be blessed, and may a fire be kindled in your mind as you seek to be successful in God! May you be challenged and inspired to live the great life with true greatness!

The seeds of greatness that need to be reproduced in our life sprout from Jesus Christ. "Reproducing the life of Jesus is life's finest, sweetest, biggest business. The Master will build the atmosphere of your life. He will make your life like a garden of roses, like an island of spices. He will bring interesting experiences, great books, inspiring sermons, rich friendships and sweet meditations into your life."[1]

The challenge is to become like Him and to be successful and prosperous in God's eyes!

Never Give Up

Dream a dream
Climb every mountain and win
Drink the nectar of life and live
Overcome obstacles and become
Taste the sweetness of victory
Dance in the sunshine of attainment
Go forward when you want to go backward
Live with fire inside your soul
Experience the impossible
Whatever you do: Never Give Up!
Only the losers give up.
                    —JOY HANEY

1
OPPORTUNITY SURROUNDS YOU: THINK!

"As we have therefore opportunity, let us do good unto all men" (Galatians 6:10).

A seed of opportunity lies in the challenge of each new day: the opportunity to love, to live, to help others, and to succeed. An opportunity should not be looked upon as only a vessel to sail towards success but as a substance to enrich lives: ours and others'. If an opportunity is squandered or lost, do not despair for long, for other opportunities will present themselves. It may not be the same opportunity, but definitely there will be more.

Life is too short to bewail the fact that an opportunity has been lost. Today is the opportunity that is given to each of us. We will either take advantage of it or cast it upon the heap of lost opportunities. The choice is up to us.

OPPORTUNITY

They do me wrong who say I come no more
When once I knock and fail to find you in;
For every day I stand outside your door
And bid you wake, and rise to fight and win.
                    —WALTER MALONE (1866-1915)[2]
American poet

15

Every day is a new opportunity: golden moments that vibrate with invitation for those with brave hearts to go forward, seize them, and win! Those who are aware and vigilant see unnoticed opportunities ignored by thousands of half-awake human beings.

Life's road can be paved with good intentions or opportunities well taken. We can make excuses and give up when the going gets rough, or we can choose to make good our intentions—doing our best with what we have and not giving up. It is easy to walk numbly through life in a daze of mediocrity, not thinking of the seed of opportunity that is half hidden under the pile of debris of unattractive situations. We must learn to think and to concentrate beyond what is evident before us.

> *Concentration is my motto—first honesty, then industry, then concentration.*
> — ANDREW CARNEGIE (1835-1919)
> Steel manufacturer and philanthropist

As setbacks make their way into the corridors of our life's story, we can continually look back at the negative past and because of this fail to see what is taking place ahead of us. Life is not always pleasant; things happen that we wish would disappear and go away. If we had the power to erase some things from ever taking place, we would all be very busy with our erasers.

> *When one door closes, another opens; but we often look so long and so regretfully upon the closed door that we do not see the one which has opened for us.*[3]
> — ALEXANDER GRAHAM BELL (1847-1922)
> American scientist and inventor

The author of this saying, Alexander Graham Bell, was born in Edinburgh, Scotland. He was twenty-seven years old when he worked out the principle of transmitting speech electrically and was twenty-nine when his basic telephone patent was granted in 1876.

His great invention was the result of many years of scientific training. Bell gained knowledge of the way sounds of speech and music are produced and heard through his training. Before this discovery, tragedy struck the Bell family. Graham's younger brother had died of tuberculosis, and his elder brother died from the same disease in 1870. The doctors gave warning that Graham, too, was threatened. His father sacrificed his career in London and, in August 1870, moved the family to Brantford, Ontario, Canada, where he found during his travels what he considered a healthy climate. While he was in Canada, Graham quickly recovered his health.

He soon began to work on his experiment but found that he lacked the time and skill to make all the necessary parts for the experiments. He went to an electrical shop for help. Thomas A. Watson began to assist Bell, and the two became fast friends.

During the tedious experiments that followed, Bell reasoned that it would be possible to pick up all the sounds of the human voice on the harmonic telegraph. Then, on June 2, 1875, while Bell was at one end of the line and Watson worked on the reeds of the telegraph in another room, Bell heard the sound of a plucked reed coming to him over the wire. Quickly he ran to Watson, shouting, "Watson, what did you do then? Don't change anything."

After an hour or so of plucking reeds and listening to the sounds, Bell gave his assistant instructions for making the "first Bell telephone." The instrument transmitted the sound of Bell's voice to Watson on the next day. The instrument transmitted recognizable voice sounds, not words. Bell and Watson experimented all summer, and in September 1875, Bell began to write the specifications for his first telephone patent.

The patent was issued on March 7, 1876. The telephone carried its first intelligible sentence three days later in the rented top floor of a Boston boardinghouse. Bell and Watson, in different rooms, were about to try a new transmitter. Then Watson heard Bell's voice saying, "Mr. Watson, come here. I want you!" Bell had upset the acid of a battery over his clothes, but he quickly forgot the accident in his excitement over the success of the new transmitter.

Bell exhibited his telephones at the Centennial Exposition in Philadelphia in June 1876. The British scientist, Sir William Thomson, called the telephone "the most wonderful thing in America."

Bell and Watson gave many successful demonstrations of the telephone, and their work paved the way for the beginning of telephone service in America. The first telephone company, the Bell Telephone Company, came into existence on July 9, 1877. Bell became an American citizen in 1882.

Many times, in order to take advantage of an opportunity, a person must leave the secure nest of sameness and daily rituals.

Some opportunities force us to veer from our well-laid schedules and to venture into an adventure. It is not easy to make changes or to undertake a new project. Comfort beckons, and we are tempted to rest easily on the cushions of the familiar.

> *Too many people are thinking of security instead of opportunity.*
> —JAMES F. BYRNES (1879-1979)
> Secretary of State under President Harry S. Truman

James Byrnes served as a Democratic representative from South Carolina in Congress from 1911 to 1925 and as a U.S. Senator from 1931 to 1941. He became an associate justice of the Supreme Court of the United States in 1941 and served until 1942, when he became head of the Office of War Mobilization. He served as governor of South Carolina from 1951 to 1955.

Rev. Billy Graham spoke of Byrnes highly: "Governor Byrnes was one of the greatest and most wonderful men I ever had the privilege of meeting. He was one of the greatest statesmen in American history." He did not get there by simply wishing but by seizing each opportunity, no matter how much work was involved.

Who knows what people will do with their lives? To each person comes certain opportunities; whether or not they take advantage of what is given them is an individual decision. Some young people feel the pressure to do things now and often fret when they are unable to accomplish what they feel is required of them when they see what everyone else around them is accomplishing.

The thing to do is to do the the best you can do and despair not, for many great works were done after people turned fifty, or even sixty, seventy, or eighty years of age. Opportunities keep coming in life. Only those who are aware of them seize them, or those who have lived a life of self-discipline, and when they are older still have the fire burning in them to give in order to leave something with the generation coming behind them. Some examples of those who did their greatest works in their later years are as follows:

- *Gladstone* was still a potential figure in political and intellectual circles when he was eighty. He took up a new language at seventy.
- *Lamarck* at seventy-eight completed his great zoological work, *The Natural History of the Invertebrates.*
- *Kelly* continued to be a cancer specialist when past eighty.
- *Franklin* did not begin his philosophical pursuits until fifty.

He went to France in the service of his country at seventy-eight and wrote his autobiography at over eighty.

- *Vanderbilt* increased the mileage of his ocean liners from one hundred to more than ten thousand between his seventieth year and his death at eighty-three and thus added over $100 million to his fortune.
- *T.W. Barnes* continued to preach when he was in his nineties.
- *Bacon* was sixty before he wrote his greatest works.
- *Milton* completed *Paradise Lost* when fifty-seven and *Paradise Regained* at sixty-three.
- *Tennyson* published "Crossing the Bar" at eighty-three.
- *Van Goethe* wrote a part of *Faust* at sixty and finished it at eighty-two.
- *Olive Wendell Holmes* at seventy-nine wrote *Over the Teacups*.
- *T.R. McDonald* ran a successful business and operated a backhoe in his eighties.
- *Victor Hugo* wrote *Les Miserables* at sixty-two.
- *George Bernard Shaw* wrote some of his famous plays at eighty.
- *Scott* the commentator began his study of Hebrew at eighty-seven.
- *Croce* the Italian philosopher published two of his works on philosophy at age eighty-five.
- *Webster* wrote his monumental dictionary at seventy.
- *John Wesley* traveled two hundred and fifty miles a day for forty years; preached forty thousand sermons; produced four hundred books; knew ten languages. At eighty-three he was annoyed that he could not write more than fifteen hours a day without hurting his eyes; and at eighty-six he was ashamed he could not preach more than twice a day. He complained in his diary that there was an increasing tendency to lie in bed until 5:30 in the morning.[4]
- *Moses* was eighty when God called, and although he cited many excuses, he never mentioned his old age.[5]
- *Socrates* gave the world his wisest philosophy at seventy and at an extreme old age learned to play on musical instruments.
- *Michelangelo* was still composing poetry and designing structures in his eighty-ninth year. He painted the ceiling

of the Sistine Chapel on his back on a scaffold at near ninety.

- *Strauss* was still composing serious music after his eightieth birthday.
- *Haydn* wrote his oratorio *The Creation* after he was sixty-seven.
- *Phillips Brooks,* one of the world's greatest preachers, was a powerful figure at eighty-four.
- *Grandma Moses* was in her seventies when she started painting. She was Anna Mary Robertson, who became an American folk artist. She could no longer do embroidery because of arthritis, so she turned to painting. She still had the fire of creativeness within her and refused to give up just because her body would not respond to her commands.

People do not just evolve magically one day into success, but long hours of hard work and right decisions preceded them. Each person is provided with the threads for his life's work, but sometimes a person must venture forth on a dream before he sees the threads. That is when they appear and everything begins to fall into place.

> *Begin to weave and God will give the thread.*
> —GERMAN PROVERB

> *God provides thread for the work begun.*
> —JAMES HOWELL (1593-1666) [6]
> English author

When those threads of thought come, our duty is to pick up the threads and to begin to weave according to the directions. We should fix our minds on the purpose and go forward, thinking only of the good and the positive and not dwelling on the negatives. The negative thoughts will always try to come, but we must choose to raise our thoughts to a higher level.

Whenever you go out-of-doors, draw the chin in, carry the crown of the head high, and fill the lungs to the utmost; drink in the sunshine; greet your friends with a smile, and put soul into every handclasp. Do not fear being misunderstood and do not waste a minute thinking about your ene-

mies. Try to fix firmly in your mind what you would like to do; and then, without veering off direction, you will move straight to the goal. Keep your mind on the great and splendid things you would like to do, and then, as the days go gliding away, you will find yourself unconsciously seizing upon the opportunities that are the fulfillment of your desire, just as the coral insect takes from the running tide the element it needs. Picture in your mind the able, earnest, useful person you desire to be, and the thought you hold is hourly transforming you into that particular individual.

— ELBERT HUBBARD (1856-1815)[7]

American "inspirational" essayist and publisher

SUCCESS STORY:

CLARENCE BIRDSEYE:

Clarence Birdseye was born in Brooklyn, New York, on December 9, 1886. When he was ten years old, his deep desire for a shotgun forced him to look for a way to earn money. His family spent their summers on a farm on Long Island. One day while he was tramping through the fields studying wildlife, he wondered if he couldn't earn some money trapping the plentiful muskrats. He wrote to the zoo in New York and asked if they could use these animals. They replied that they could not, but they sent him the name of a man who wanted twelve of them to stock his farm. He filled the order immediately. With the sale of these muskrats at one dollar each, he earned enough to buy his gun. This was his first venture. Since that time, by keeping his eyes open and his mind working, he has done much to make life more pleasant for thousands and has earned a fortune for himself.

When in Amherst College he earned $115 by catching frogs in a nearby pond and selling them to the zoo for snake food. Later he earned $135, selling to a geneticist the rare black rats found in a storage shed back of the Amherst butcher shop. Still later, while on vacation, he made $600 selling bobcat and coyote skins.

When he was twenty-six, he left a well-paying job to see if silver foxes could be transplanted to the United States as breeding stock. In spite of these plans going awry (because Newfoundland passed a law prohibiting the exportation of live foxes from Labrador), he still made $6,000 that year trapping foxes for a fur company.

At the end of his year in Labrador, he came back to the States

21

and was married, then moved his new bride back to Labrador. Living in a primitive society and lacking the conveniences of refrigeration, they were compelled to preserve their food by freezing it outside their cabin. They soon learned that the faster it was frozen, the better the taste when it came to the table. Cutting paper-thin slices from the frozen foods, Mr. Birdseye discovered that the quick frozen flesh was firm while the meat which was frozen slower had large ice crystals in the flesh and leaked juice when thawed.

He came back to the United States and went into the fish business. It was here he began to think about the commercial possibilities of freezing fish and became the founder of frozen fish. This was the start of the Birdseye frozen foods, which have changed the eating habits of a nation. First he started freezing fish; then he found that this same method could also be used to preserve all kinds of food, actually keeping them fresher than any other method. In 1929, he sold out the frozen food business for $22 million.

Clarence Birdseye did not retire in the usual sense. He was still asking questions and finding answers. He found a new way to simplify and to speed up the manufacture of paper. He invented an automatic electric reel for fishermen. He also experimented in gardening and believed that in the future a gardener would need only a few feet of ground to grow all he could eat.

SUCCESS NUGGETS:

To improve the golden moment of opportunity and catch the good that is within our reach, is the great art of life.
—SAMUEL JOHNSON[8]

A wise man will make more opportunities than he finds.
—FRANCIS BACON (1561-1626)
English philosopher, statesman, and author

THE WAYS

To every man there openeth
A Way, and Ways, and a Way
And the High Soul climbs the High Way,
And the Low Soul gropes the Low,
And in between, on the misty flats,

The rest drift to and fro.

But to every man there openeth
A High Way, and a Low.
And every man decideth
The way his soul shall go.
— JOHN OXENHAM[9]

Men were born to succeed, not to fail.
— HENRY DAVID THOREAU[10]

2
ONE MUST TAKE
RISKS TO SUCCEED

"And the LORD said unto Moses, Wherefore criest thou
unto me? speak unto the children of Israel, that they go forward"
(Exodus 14:15).

The children of Israel were in crisis. The enemy was chasing
them from behind, and the great Red Sea was before them. God
thundered, "Go forward!" This was a risk! Would God keep them
from drowning? Moses took the risk and stretched his rod over the
Red Sea, and God performed a miracle, parted the sea, and sent a
wind to dry the muddy ground until it became a dry path for them
to walk to the other side.

Ask the early explorers: Marco Polo, Lewis and Clark, Magel-
lan. Ask the scientists who brought to the world medicines that
would cure. Ask the missionaries who went forth to foreign countries. Ask the inventors. Ask them all the same question, "Was it a
risk?" and they will all answer with a resounding tone, "Yes, there
were many risks!"

*Every noble acquisition is attended with its risks; he who fears to en-
counter the one must not expect to obtain the other.*
— PIETRO METASTASIO (1698-1782)
Italian poet and librettist He succeeded Apostolo Zeno as poet
laureate at the imperial court of Vienna (1730-82).

Does taking risks mean there will be no mistakes? Far from this—there will be many wrong turns, wrong judgments, failure to go a certain way, but the guiding force that urged the risk taker in the first place will steer him back to the right turn, the right judgment, the right way. Life is not about *not* making mistakes; it should be about living life to the fullest and arriving at our destination successfully.

> *He who never made a mistake never made a discovery.*
> —SAMUEL SMILES (1812-1904)
> English writer

EXAMPLE OF THIS:

LOUIS PASTEUR

Louis Pasteur (1822-1895) of France was one of the world's greatest scientists. He made major contributions to chemistry, medicine, and industry that have greatly benefited mankind. His discovery that bacteria spread diseases saved and is saving countless lives.

Louis was born the son of a tanner in Dole, France. The family soon moved to Arbois, where he received his early education. Pasteur was a slow but careful student who showed a talent for art. He later studied chemistry at the Ecole Normale and the Sorbonne in Paris. In 1849, he became a science professor in Strasbourg, France, where he began studying fermentation, a type of chemical breakdown of substances by microbes.

In 1860, at a doctor's office in Paris, Pasteur stated that dirty hands caused childbed fever. Pasteur told the doctors at the hospital: "Wash your hands. Boil your instruments. Microbes cause disease and death to your patients."

They were outraged. They said about him, "He is a menace to science. If he is allowed to continue, he will make the practice of medicine unsafe for us physicians and surgeons of France."

Someone else asked, "How does he know? He is not a doctor, sir; he is a mere chemist."

Many people who went to the hospital experienced death. Pasteur's answer: "Criminal disregard of germs and their power to invade the bloodstream is causing a death rate in childbirth alone of three out of every ten mothers, or in the city of Paris over twenty thousand innocent and helpless women annually."

He worked countless hours in his laboratory, trying again, again, and again. His aim: "Find the microbe; kill the microbe that was causing the death." Doctors could not believe that a human being could be destroyed by an organism ten thousand times smaller than a flea. It became such a battle between doctors and Pasteur that he was invited to visit Emperor Napoleon of France. While there he was ridiculed and forbidden by the emperor to study medicine or to continue his study of microbes.

He went home from that meeting with news to his wife that he was leaving Paris the very next day. They moved back to Arbois, where he had studied as a boy. Soon after, in 1870 the Franco-Prussian War broke out. While that war was being fought, Pasteur was fighting microbes.

After the war, Louis Adolphe Thiers replaced the emperor as the First President of the Republic of France. Under his reign, the people were forced to pay 5 million francs. France was suffering not only from the ravages of war but also from a deadly plague called the Black Plague. At a government meeting, one of the counselors told the new president that all of France was affected by the plague except one province called Arbois. He said, "If there is no disease among the sheep of Arbois, it is our duty to find out why. Every animal that you can save will buy back some Frenchman's liberty and self-respect." The President ordered a thorough investigation. They found Louis Pasteur vaccinating sheep. They scoffed at him, but one young doctor, Dr. Martell, believed in him.

The doctor who was appointed by the president went back to Paris and published in the paper the following: "No anthrax in Arbois. Radisse urges farmers to bring healthy sheep to Arbois at expense of state. The government moved in, took some of the grazing land and sheep came by the thousands."

This resulted in a contract between Pasteur and the government at Pouilly LeFont. All sheep would be given an injection of the blood of diseased sheep that had died. However, Pasteur vaccinated twenty-five with anthrax. People came by the thousands from all over to Europe to laugh and to mock him. Pasteur became a laughingstock. Even one of his enemies, Dr. Lister from England, came, but not to laugh. He was interested in the experiment.

Pasteur won. All sheep died except those vaccinated by him. Dr. Lister said to him, "If I've been skeptical, I beg you to forgive me. It's a miracle."

Pasteur's next challenge was finding a vaccine for rabies, a deadly disease spread by the bite of mad dogs (rabies-infected animals). In 1882, Pasteur went back to Paris, and when his wife objected to his bringing a mad dog into the laboratory, he said, "I've pledged myself to find a cure. I can't stop now, not until I've exhausted every effort to rid the world of this deadly disease."

The newspapers picked up his claim, "To rid the world of hydrophobia—claims disease due to microbe."

When they brought Joseph Meister to him, a small boy who had been bitten by a mad dog, he had to choose if he would take a chance. If he lost, it could mean prison or the guillotine for him. He decided to take a chance. The boy became a test case. After several weeks of treatment, the vaccine proved successful. The boy did not get rabies.

The Russian embassy sent hundreds of peasants that had been bitten, to offer themselves as test cases. "Take them to the hospital; isolate them. I want a full report on every case." He cured many of these patients also.

Although Pasteur was successful, he faced continual opposition. Even in 1886, controversies still surrounded Pasteur. In the corridors of the Academy of Sciences, there were cries: "Pasteur is a murderer!"[11]

Toward the end of his life, the government hosted a big celebration to honor Pasteur. The Imperial Majesty, the czar of Russia, gave him recognition and a necklace for the role he played in his studies with rabies. He was honored by all the leading physicians and chemists. He won because he was willing to take risks and to follow what he knew to be right. The following paragraph is an excerpt of the speech he made at this occasion:

> *Young people, young people, have faith in those sure and powerful methods whose first secrets we are just beginning to understand. All of you, whatever your future career, do not let yourself to be touched by denigrating and sterile skepticism, and do not become discouraged by the sadness of certain hours that a nation has to experience. Do not become angry at your opponents, for no scientific*

theory has been accepted without opposition.

If Pasteur had continued doing his normal job and had not pursued the fire of his ideas, he would have stayed in what is called a rut: doing the same thing over and over without reaching, finding, and improving.

Ruts become a premature grave. They are safe places, but they smell of boredom and depict lackluster lives. No one ever ventured far from a grave unless there was a supernatural resurrection. There is no chance for failure in a rut, but neither is there hope for success.

> *You won't skid if you stay in a rut.*
> — KIN HUBBARD (1868-1930)
> American humorist and writer

Just begin to do what you want to do, and somehow the components needed to make the venture a success will appear. If you wait for everything to be in place before you venture forth, you will be waiting a very long time.

So what if the road to success is dangerous and the storms of life batter the ship! The journey into the storm is worth it if you are truly living and are doing what you were born to do.

> *The fishermen know that the sea is dangerous and the storm terrible, but they have never found these dangers sufficient reason for remaining ashore.*
> — VINCENT VAN GOGH (1853-1890)
> Dutch painter

Life is a venture. We should all sail forth doing great deeds and following our dreams. The gift of life should be savored, but at the same time, it should be invested in something worthwhile, helping others to find their way. Why were we born? Can we sit safely in a harbor when we were destined to sail?

> *A ship in harbor is safe, but that is not what ships are built for.*
> — JOHN A. SHEDD, (1859-?)
> American author

Life is not worth living if we do not sail forth into our destiny. To merely exist day after day in a hole of self-misery, doing nothing but going through the motions as a rat in a cage, is the most despicable kind of life. This is the day to venture forth even if it is toward something we have never done before. The first step is the beginning of the rest of our lives.

> *Life is either a daring adventure, or nothing.*
> — AUTHOR UNKNOWN

EXAMPLE OF THIS:

At a meeting in London, Winston Churchill gave the story of his escape from a South African military prison in Pretoria. Churchill told how, after wandering in the region around Pretoria for two or three days and feeling at the end of his tether, he made up his mind to present himself at the door of one of the houses whose lights were twinkling in the valley below.

Although a price had been set upon his head, he thought there was a chance of some friendly soul in the heart of that enemy country, and he prayed earnestly that he might be guided to the right house. Then he went to the door of one of the houses and knocked. A man opened the door and asked what he wanted.

"I am Winston Churchill," he replied.

"Come in," said the friendly voice. "This is the only house for miles in which you would be safe."[12]

Churchill took a risk and won. He prayed, and God heard his prayer and led him to the right house. He was forced to make a shot in the dark, but divine guidance helped him make the right shot. If he had not taken the shot, he probably would have been captured, and history would have been written entirely differently.

> *You will always miss 100 percent of the shots you don't take.*
> — AUTHOR UNKNOWN

Andrew Carnegie, the successful steel magnate, was known to take risks. In his book, *Empire of Business*, he wrote that he was "chiefly dependent for his revenues not upon salary but upon profits. . . . The businessman pure and simple plunges into and tosses upon the waves of human affairs without a life-preserver in the shape of salary; he risks all."[13]

It takes faith to embark upon a new life, a new discovery, or a new experiment, but it is worth it. Life was not meant to live in fear and in a cowering position. Someone once said, "I would rather walk with God by faith, than walk alone by sight." Go with God! Do the impossible through Christ. Reach your dreams in faith!

The human soul must be willing to step forward and to go forth in a blaze of determination and excitement, reaching for that which it desires.

> *The willingness to take risks is our grasp of faith.*
> —GEORGE E. WOODBERRY (1855-1930)
> American poet, critic, and educator

EXAMPLE OF THIS:

PAUL EHRLICH

Ehrlich (1854-1915) was a German bacteriologist. He founded modern hematology by developing techniques for staining the various types of blood corpuscles. He also worked at increasing immunity to disease, including the development of diphtheria antitoxin.

While working as a doctor at a hospital, he was willing to go against tradition. He became known for discovering salvarson, a remedy for syphilis. It is called "606" because it was the 606th compound tested. During the tests, he suffered the scorn of his colleagues, and his budget was cut off by the elite medical society.

They threatened to make him leave the hospital, but Ehrlich fought back. He said, "If you make me leave this hospital before I treat these children, I will tell these mothers."

It was a relief to him when, after several days, one of the nurses told him, "Every one of the children you injected are saved!" After this critical test, there was one person who believed in him and gave him money for him to pursue his studies.

The other doctors laughed at him when he tried to find serum to fight human diseases, but he worked in spite of their jeering. After finding immunity for diphtheria, he was asked by one of his superiors, "Now I want you to establish a serum for typhoid."

In 1882 Ehrlich began work with Koch, whose specialty was tuberculosis. Unfortunately, he caught a light case of the disease in 1886 and had to retire to Egypt, where he hoped the dry climate might cure him. It did, and while there he found a serum for snakebite.

In 1908 Ehrlich was awarded a share, along with Mechnikow, of the Nobel Prize in medicine and physiology for his work on immunity and serum therapy generally. As was to happen in more than one case, however, his most dramatic achievement came after the Nobel Prize.

In 1909 a new assistant of Ehrlich picked up chemical 606

again. (By now Ehrlich had reached the 900s.) It was still no good for trypanosomes, but it turned out to be a remarkably efficient killer for spirochetes, the microorganism that causes syphilis.

Ehrlich named the chemical salvarsan (although its proper short chemical name is now arshenamine). For the rest of his life, he worked strenuously to see that the medical profession used the chemical correctly. He had 65,000 units distributed to physicians all over the globe without charge, feeling the cure to be more important than income.

Sometimes doctors did not follow instructions carefully, and incorrect usage led to tragedies that brought vicious attacks on Ehrlich as a quack and a murderer. Ehrlich won, however (though he was forced to sue the most slanderous ones), and shone the more brightly and permanently as a healer and benefactor of mankind.

If you could bring Ehrlich from the grave and ask him if it was worth taking a risk to save other lives, he would firmly vow that it was worth it. Risk taking is associated with all things that are worthwhile. The desire to do the right thing is greater than the risks.

Risk taking has always been in the heart of the successful ones. It was Abraham, the father of the Jewish nation, who left his country for an unknown place simply because God told him to do so. Christopher Columbus sailed unknown seas to prove his theory that the world was round. The Wright brothers were willing to be called crazy in order to prove that airplanes could fly. These men had no securities other than a dream, a voice, a theory, or a feeling. It has been from the beginning and always will be — in order to forge ahead to new horizons, risks must be taken.

> *Every year I live I am more convinced that the waste of life lies in the love we have not given, the powers we have not used, the selfish prudence that will risk nothing, and which, shirking pain, misses happiness as well. No one ever yet was the poorer in the long run for having once in a lifetime "let out all the length of all the reins."*
> — MARY CHOLMONDELEY[14]

SUCCESS STORY:

HARRIET TUBMAN

Harriet Tubman, a famous figure in American Civil War history, was a "conductor" of the Underground Railroad, a network of people, black and white, who helped slaves escape from the South into the free North and Canada by offering them safe hiding places and food.

Harriet Green was born into slavery in 1815 and worked on a plantation on the eastern shore of Maryland, serving as nurse-maid, field hand, and cook. The master often criticized her work and treated her harshly. One day, when she was thirteen, Harriet was ordered by an overseer to help tie up another slave, who was to be whipped for going into town without permission. Harriet refused. The overseer picked up a two-pound iron weight and hurled it at the truant slave. It missed and instead hit Harriet in the head, fracturing her skull. The injury caused Harriet to experience periods of uncontrolled sleepiness and even blackouts for the rest of her life.

In 1844, Harriet married another slave, John Tubman. When the owner of the plantation died in 1849, rumor circulated that Harriet would be sold to a plantation in another state. It was then that she made the decision to escape to one of the eighteen free northern states.

She said, "I had reasoned this out in my mind; there was one of two things I had a *right* to, liberty or death; if I could not have one, I would have the other; for no man should take me alive; I should fight for my liberty as long as my strength lasted, and when the time came for me to go, the Lord would let them take me."[15]

When she reached the Mason-Dixon line, the boundary between Delaware and Pennsylvania that divided the slave states from the free states, she said, "I looked at my hands to see if I was the same person now I was free. There was such glory over everything, the sun came like gold through the trees, and over the fields, and I felt like I was in heaven."[16]

Her ecstasy was soon replaced with the harsh reality of her situation. Harriet lived in Philadelphia for one year, working hard in hotels, saving money, and thinking about her family back home. When she heard that her sister and her two children were going to be sold to another plantation, she returned south to help them escape. They traveled by wagon, boat, and foot, hiding in barns and other safe places along the route that became known as the Underground Railroad.

In the decade preceding the Civil War, Harriet helped more than three hundred people gain their freedom. Even though she was considered an outlaw and a fugitive, she always escaped her pursuers. She knew that, under the Fugitive Slave Act, she could be punished or killed if she was caught, but she also knew that she had to take the risk. She once said, "On my underground railroad I never ran my train off the track and I never lost a passenger."

She stoked up their courage by leading them in the hymn, "Go down Moses; go down to the Promised Land." Harriet became known as "the Moses of her people." Ann Petry described her leadership thus: "Though she was not aware of it, she had become a legend in the slave cabins along the Eastern Shore. She had always had the makings of a legend in her: the prodigious strength, the fearlessness, the religious ardor, the visions she had in which she experienced moments of prescience. . . . The slaves said she could see in the dark like a mule; that she could smell danger down the wind like a fox; that she could move through thick underbrush without making a sound, like a field mouse. They said she was so strong she could pick up a grown man, sling him over her shoulder, and walk with him for miles. . . .They said, voices muted, awed, that she talked with God every day, just like Moses. They said there was some strange power in her so that no one could die when she was with them. She enveloped the sick and the dying with her strength, sending it from her body to theirs, sustaining them."

For the times when a slave became frightened and wanted to leave to return back home, she carried a gun with her to use as a threat. If one of the runaways said, "Let me go back," and would turn away, saying, "I'm going back," she would aim the revolver at him and say, "Go on with us or die." She would say, "We got to go free or die. And freedom's not bought with dust."

During the War between the States, Harriet served the Union as scout, spy, and nurse. After the war, she helped to establish schools for blacks, joined the women's suffrage movement, and created a rest home for the aged Negroes.

Harried died in 1913 of pneumonia. She was "a short, indomitable woman, sustained by faith in a living God, inspired by her belief that freedom was a right all men should enjoy, leading bands of trembling fugitives out of Tidewater Maryland."

Her friend Frederick Douglass, the abolitionist and founder of the American Anti-Slavery Society, summed up Harriet Tubman's life best in a letter to her: "I know of no one who has willingly encountered more perils and hardships to serve our enslaved people than you have."

SUCCESS NUGGETS:

I have lived eighty-six years. I have watched men climb up to success, hundreds of them, and of all the elements that are important for success, the most important is faith. No great thing comes to any man unless he has courage.
— CARDINAL JAMES BIGGONS[17]

Cowards die many times before their deaths. The valiant never taste of death but once.
— WILLIAM SHAKESPEARE[18]

The fact is, that to do anything in the world worth doing, we must not stand back shivering and thinking of the cold and danger, but jump in and scramble through as well as we can. It will not do to be perpetually calculating risks and adjusting nice chances.
— SIDNEY SMITH[19]

While we stop to think, we often miss our opportunity.
— PUBLIUS SYRUS

3

FAILURE: THE STEPPING-STONE TO GREATER THINGS

"But I have prayed for thee, that thy faith fail not" (Luke 22:32).

Jesus knew Peter was going to fail Him, but He was more concerned about his faith than his failure. Peter did fail and wept bitterly, but he did not give in to self-pity and defeat. Instead he strengthened his faith and became a mighty apostle in God's kingdom.

Failure does not mean that all is lost or that life is over. It just signifies that one part of life's venture is finished, but a whole new future is waiting for those who just get up and start over. It is now time for new plans and schemes or even a polishing of old dreams. Failure can be the best thing that ever happened, for it is through tears and hardship that one can see further than when the bright lights dim his vision. There is always tomorrow, always a fresh start, always a new day in which to look forward.

When all else is lost, the future still remains.
— CHRISTIAN NESTELL BOVEE (1820-1904)
American writer

The end many times is just the beginning of something better. The lesson learned from a venture failed is priceless knowledge for future investments and actions. Most successful people fail more than once, sometimes many times before they succeed. It has often been said, "Today's success was twenty-five years in the making." And in those years, there were failures, heartaches, and disappointments, but those failures did not rule life. They were never the end; they were only the beginning.

> *The world is round and the place which may seem like the end may also be only the beginning.*
> — IVY BAKER PRIEST (1905-1975)
> US Treasurer

The first attempt of David Livingstone to preach ended in failure. "Friends, I have forgotten all I had to say," he gasped and in shame stepped from the pulpit. At that moment Robert Moffat, who was visiting Edinburgh, advised David not to give up. He suggested perhaps he could be a doctor instead of a preacher. Livingstone decided to be both. When the years of medical study were done, he went to Africa.

Livingstone, born in Scotland in 1813, was one of the most popular national heroes of the nineteenth century. He became a successful medical missionary and explorer in South Africa.

Even if it seems like life's opportunity is over, just have patience, for patience in any venture will bear fruit. It just takes time for things to come to fruition. So do as the poet said: dry the eyes, get up, and begin again.

> *To dry one's eyes and laugh at a fall,*
> *And baffled, get up and begin again.*
> — ROBERT BROWNING (1812-1889)
> English poet

The great preacher, Phillips Brooks, at first failed at what he did. After graduating from Harvard College, he taught school but could not seem to make a go of it and in time was forced to resign his position. Charles Francis Adams wrote that the young man was "humiliated, discouraged, utterly broken down, indeed, by his complete failure at the threshold of his life." Another biographer, Alexander V. G. Allen says: "It was a catastrophe, complete, final, and humiliating. The headmaster had offered consolation to Brooks after his discomfiture in the remark that he had never known any-one who failed as schoolmaster to succeed in any other calling. It was an event calling for comment among a large circle of acquaintances, who had expected great things. Nothing was wanting to make the sense of mortification complete. Fortunately he was able to rouse himself. Once more ambition took possession of him. Six months after his resignation he entered the theological seminary, and three years later he began his career in the pulpit that made him famous."[20]

What if he had succeeded as a schoolmaster? What if those who called themselves his friends had succeeded in their thoughtless campaign to brand him a failure for life?

Patience is a virtue. Seek to add this to your new list of attainments in the times of failure and tears, for good things come to those who learn to wait. One cannot rush results, but they will come in their own time. Do what is right and work toward reaching a goal without becoming frustrated, and in time, the obscure will be made clear.

All beginnings are somewhat strange, but we must have patience, and, little by little, we shall find things, which at first were obscure, becoming clear.
— VINCENT DE PAUL (1580-1660)
French missionary

Defeat is never the end but is just the beginning of success. How can we know what works and what doesn't if we never fail? Life is learning one step at a time, an experiment here, a crossing-out of that, and an adding of this. Life can be likened to a scientist's lab. If this doesn't work, there will eventually be something that does.

What is defeat? Nothing but education, nothing but the first step to something better.
— WENDELL PHILLIPS (1811-1884)
Orator and reformer

Defeat can cause one to become stronger, giving him a greater resolution to win and making him more disciplined in his quest. It is not about losing; it is about learning, becoming resilient and fearless. It is the strong who have failed but refused to let failure be their soul mate. They have risen with new goals, new plans, and excitement for the future. Successful people refuse to give up or give in to their circumstances. They are only made better.

> *It is defeat that turns bone to flint; it is defeat that turns gristle to muscle; it is defeat that makes men invincible.*
> —HENRY WARD BEECHER (1813-1887)
> Eloquent, dramatic, and witty Protestant preacher and author

Failure is but a malfunction that needs work applied to it. Look upon failure as the material to build upon an edifice of success. Sift through the pile of broken dreams, failed plans, or disappointments, and look for something that is salvageable. Pick it up, brush it off, look at it long and hard, and begin again.

> *There is no failure except in no longer trying. There is no defeat except from within, no really insurmountable barrier save our own inherent weakness of purpose.*
> —KIN HUBBARD (pen name) (1868-1930)
> Frank McKinney Hubbard, American author, humorist, and
> journalist He wrote as philosopher under the title "Abe Martin."

We all receive signals from within and from without. Listen to the signals that call you to attention to move forward. Disregard signals that send you spiraling back into the abyss of failure. Defeat can be a signal to press forward and not opt out of life prematurely, for it is a time of reflection. Learn to reflect positively concerning all things that bother you and to push away the things that are defeating you. To which signals do you allow yourself to listen?

> *Defeat is simply a signal to press onward.*
> —HELEN KELLER (1889-1968)[21]
> Deaf and blind speaker and author

Although Helen was deaf and blind, Anne Sullivan taught her a language she could speak. She went to college and learned not only the English language but also spoke in German and French. She became a speaker, author, and crusader for the deaf.

The following is a portion of Helen's address at the fifth meeting of the American Association to promote the teaching of speech to the deaf, at Mt. Airy, Philadelphia, Pennsylvania, July 8, 1896:

I can remember the time before I learned to speak, and how I used to struggle to express my thoughts by means of the manual alphabet—how my thoughts used to beat against my finger tips like little birds striving to gain their freedom, until one day Miss Fuller opened wide the prison-door and let them escape. I wonder if she remembers how eagerly and gladly they spread their wings and flew away. Of course, it was not easy at first to fly. The speech-wings were weak and broken, and had lost all the grace and beauty that had once been theirs; indeed, nothing was left save the impulse to fly, but that was something. One can never consent to creep when one feels an impulse to soar. But, nevertheless, it seemed to me sometimes that I could never use my speech-wings as God intended I should use them; there were so many difficulties in the way, so many discouragements; but I kept on trying, knowing that patience and perseverance would win in the end.

And while I worked, I built the most beautiful air-castles, and dreamed dreams, the pleasantest of which was of the time when I should talk like other people; and the thought of the pleasure it would give my mother to hear my voice once more, sweetened every effort and made every failure an incentive to try harder next time.

So I want to say to those who are trying to learn to speak and those who are teaching them: Be of good cheer. Do not think of today's failures, but of the success that may come tomorrow. You have set yourselves a difficult task, but you will succeed if you persevere; and you will find a joy in overcoming obstacles—a delight in climbing rugged paths, which you would perhaps never know if you did not sometime slip backward—if the road was always smooth and pleasant. Remember, no effort that we make to attain something beautiful is ever lost. Sometime, somewhere, somehow we shall find that which we seek. We shall speak, yes, and sing, too, as God intended we should speak and sing.[22]

To be able to delight in climbing rugged paths requires a change of mind and a new way of looking at things. When the mind is soaring but the situations around you remain mundane and you feel helpless in reaching your dreams, that is the time to remember that there will come a time when the helplessness will leave, and your dreams will come to pass.

Fight valiantly against discouragement, for this is the enemy of success. You were created to win; to dare to dream is your God-given prerogative. Grow instead of wilting in the face of difficulty and, yes, even failure.

> *Difficulties are meant to rouse, not discourage. The human spirit is to grow strong by conflict.*
>   — WILLIAM ELLERY CHANNING (1780-1842)[23]
>   American clergyman

It takes courage to keep fighting, even when everything dictates for you to quit. No matter what mountain stands in your way, you must just keep climbing until you reach the summit. Have courage today to reach your goal, as the following poem demonstrates:

THREE KINDS OF COURAGE

There's the courage that serves you in starting to climb
The mount of success rising sheer;
And when you've slipped back there's the courage sublime
That keeps you from shedding a tear.
These two kinds of courage, I give you my word,
Are worthy of courage — but then,
You'll not reach the summit unless you've the third —
The courage of try-it-again!
            — AUTHOR UNKNOWN[24]

Failure should be a teacher, but oft times it becomes a stumbling block and a heavy stone in the heart. The stone is so heavy that it is difficult to remove, but just because it is difficult is no reason to give up or to stop reaching toward your dream.

> *A failure teaches you that something can't be done — that way.*
>   — THOMAS ALVA EDISON (1847-1931)

This quote comes from a man who refused to give up. He tried over two thousand different ways to make a light bulb burn, and they all failed. The number of failures did not matter to him; what counted was just the process of finding the right way. Because he refused to let failure dictate to him, he finally found the formula that worked. Edison's failures were not stumbling blocks but stepping-stones to where he was destined to go.

You cannot keep a determined man from success. Place stumbling

blocks in his way, and he takes them for steppingstones.
— ORISON SWETT MARDEN (1848-1924)
Founder of the *Success* magazine

During his quest to invent the phonograph, one night a fire ignited inside Edison's plant. While he helplessly watched it burn, with his costly experiments going up in flames, he called his son Charles. "Come!" he said. "You'll never see anything like this again!" Then he called his wife. As the three stood gazing, Edison said, "There go all our mistakes. Now we can start over afresh."[25] In two weeks he started rebuilding the plant, and it was not long before he invented the phonograph. His disappointment did not destroy him; it just strengthened his resolve even more.

Disappointment to a noble soul is what cold water is to burning metal; it strengthens, tempers, intensifies, but never destroys it.
— ELIZA TABOR (1835-1914)
English author and novelist

Not only will there be disappointments in life and the bitter taste of failure, but there will be opportunity to learn from the things that went wrong. The Japanese have a saying that is true: "Failure teaches success."[26] It will teach if we will allow it to do so.

Failure is not fatal. Failure should be our teacher, not our undertaker. It should challenge us to new heights of accomplishments, not pull us to new depths of despair. From honest failure can come valuable experience.
— WILLIAM ARTHUR WARD (1921-1994)
American author, editor, pastor, and teacher

Do not give failure the satisfaction of destroying you. It is not meant to kill but to give knowledge and experience. Failure should be a challenge to reach higher heights and to go beyond failed efforts. It is not a time to stop — that is the worst thing a person can do. In spite of failing at something; just forge ahead, face life head on, and with unswerving determination.

Adversity causes some men to break; others to break records.
— WILLIAM ARTHUR WARD

Failure is not falling; it is staying down when one falls. Nobody need stay a failure! It does not matter what family someone is born into, what the environment is, or that other people expect him to fail. People were born to succeed. It just takes some people longer to find their way than others, but anyone can make it if he determines to do so. Do not be discouraged, but get up and try again.

A CREED FOR THE DISCOURAGED

I believe that God created me to be happy, to enjoy the blessings of life, to be useful to my fellow-beings, and an honor to my country.

I believe that the trials which beset me today are but the fiery tests by which my character is strengthened, ennobled and made worthy to enjoy the higher things of life, which I believe are in store for me.

I believe that my soul is too grand to be crushed by defeat; I will rise above it.

I will be master of circumstances and surroundings, not their slave.

I will not yield to discouragements. I will trample them under foot and make them serve as steppingstones to success. I will conquer my obstacles and turn them into opportunities.

My failures of today will help to guide me on to victory on the morrow.

The morrow will bring new strength, new hopes, new opportunities and new beginnings. I will be ready to meet it with a brave heart, a calm mind and an undaunted spirit.

In all things I will do my best, and leave the rest to the Infinite.

I will not waste my mental energies by useless worry. I will learn to dominate my restless thoughts and look on the bright side of things.

I will face the world bravely; I will not be a coward. For I am immortal, and nothing can overcome me.

— VIRGINIA OPAL MYERS[27]

SUCCESS STORY:

Beverly and Ruby Osborne were the first to introduce "chicken in the rough." It all started in 1936 when they were driving from the Dust Bowl in Oklahoma to California, trying to forget that they had just failed in the business they had spent a lifetime building. They were middle aged, the Depression had wiped out their savings, and both felt pretty low. With not much more than their meager belongings and a basket of fried chicken, Beverly Osborne coaxed his Ford pickup across the barren prairie.

For lunch, they ate some of the fried chicken that Ruby brought to help revive their spirits. Just then the pickup went over a bump, and the chicken scattered all over the floor. As she picked it up, she made the comment, "This is really chicken in the rough!"

Suddenly her husband was captured by an idea. He swung the car around and started back for Oklahoma City. This chance remark meant a fortune to the Osbornes. They borrowed sixty thousand dollars and built a drive-in restaurant where people were served fried chicken without knives or forks and were presented with a finger bowl instead. They served shoestring potatoes, hot biscuits, and honey with it. That was the delectable meal that started "Fast Food—Fried Chicken Franchising." The idea was an immediate success. In 1950 *Time* magazine ran a feature article on the "Chicken in the Rough" operation, and at that time the Osbornes were grossing almost $2 million a year and had sold 335 million orders of "Chicken in the Rough." By 1955 they had over 250 restaurants, including some as far away as Johannesburg, South Africa.

It all started with just a statement. A moment in time, an idea was born, it germinated, hard work was applied, and excitement followed. Before long, and as the seed or idea became full blown, it became the success that it was.

SUCCESS NUGGETS:
There are few positions in life in which difficulties have not to be encountered. These difficulties are, however, our best instructors, as our mistakes often form our best experience. We learn wisdom from failure more than from success. We often discover what will do by finding out what will not do. Great thoughts, discoveries, and inventions have very generally been nurtured in hardship, often pondered over in sorrow and established with difficulty.
— Paxton Hood[28]

Develop success from failures. Discouragement and failure are two of the surest stepping stones to success.
— Dale Carnegie

More undertakings fail for want of spirit than for want of sense.
— WILLIAM HAZLITT[29]

ISNT IT STRANGE

Isn't it strange
That princes and kings,
And clowns that caper
In sawdust rings,
And common people
Like you and me
Are builders for eternity?

Each is given a bag of tools,
A shapeless mass,
A book of rules;
And each must make —
Ere life is flown —
A stumbling block
Or a stepping-stone.
— R. L. SHARPE[30]

4

ATTITUDE
DETERMINES
ALTITUDE

"Daniel was preferred above the presidents and princes, because an excellent spirit was in him" (Daniel 6:3).

Daniel had a great attitude and lived his life on the principles of his God, and his God did not fail him when he was put in the lions' den. He was an important figure in the king's court and served several kings because he had an excellent spirit.

The world loves a winner, but what makes a winner? Much of the aura that surrounds a winner is his or her attitude. The inner conviction about his surroundings bleeds through in every situation and circumstance. Everyday people experience similar trials as someone else, but the difference in the situation is something that each one brings to what is happening. It isn't what happens to someone that determines his destiny, but it is his attitude toward it.

It is not difficulties that make or unmake our success, but our attitude toward them.
        —J. L. CHESTNUT (1930-2008)
        Lawyer, civil rights leader, and author

"Isn't it true that a lot of us blame the road when it's really just a pebble in our shoe? We think the whole road is rough and looking back over something that seemed extremely hard and rough, we wonder how we got through it so easily. The mental pebbles that we put in our shoes make the job hard—not the job itself. Once we get rid of the mental obstacle, our whole attitude is different."[31]

The following story shows how attitude is everything:

When the young salesman had been out less than a month, he was so discouraged that he was about to give up. Just then he encountered a man who had been on the road for years.

"Well, how is the selling game going?" asked the older man.

"Pretty poor," answered the younger man. "I've been insulted at nearly every place I have visited."

"That's strange," said the old timer. "I've been on the road forty years. I've had my samples flung into the street; I've been taken by the scruff of the neck and hurled down stairs. I've had doors slammed in my face time and time again, and I can't tell you the number of times I've been cursed. I'll even admit that I've been rolled in the gutter. But in all the years of my selling I can't remember ever having been insulted, not once!"[32]

It's all how you look at it that counts!

Attitude is reflected in how we react to disappointments, failure, and anything that does not go our way. You can either cry, give in to despair, or laugh, and you probably will cry a little and maybe experience a little despair. The secret is that if you can let the wells of laughter well up within you and laugh a little bit about the whole crazy thing, there will come a lifting of your spirit. Proverbs 17:22 says it will help heal you: "A merry heart doeth good like a medicine."

Dale Carnegie shares the following characteristic, which helped him to succeed, about Schwab:

> *When Charles Schwab was addressing the student body at Princeton, he confessed that one of the most important lessons he had ever learned was taught to him by an old German who worked in Schwab's steel mill. This old German got involved in a hot wartime argument with the other steelworkers, and they tossed him into the river. "When he came into my office," Mr. Schwab said, "covered with mud and water, I asked him what he had said to the men who had thrown him into the river," and he replied: "I yust laughed."*
>
> *Mr. Schwab declared that he had adopted that old German's words as his motto: "Yust laugh."*[33]

It is not just thinking success, but it is learning to laugh at hardships that will insure progress. "A sense of humor is invaluable in a time of crisis. Cheerfulness or joyfulness is the atmosphere under which all things thrive." — RICHTER[34]

Those who can smile at themselves or laugh, instead of getting angry and tense, are by far the winners in life. It was Josh Billings who once said, "[Laffing] is the fireworks of the soul."[35] So fire up the soul and waste not the day by being to tense! Shakespeare said, "They laugh that win."

The conqueror is one who has learned to laugh even at the blasts of life, as the following poem describes:

THE CONQUEROR
It's easy to laugh when the skies are blue
And the sun is shining bright;
Yes, easy to laugh when your friends are true
And there's happiness in sight;
But when hope has fled and the skies are gray,
And the friends of the past have turned away,
Ah, then indeed it's a hero's feat
To conjure a smile in the face of defeat.

It's easy to laugh when the storm is o'er
And your ship is safe in port;
Yes, easy to laugh when you're on the shore
Secure from the tempest's sport;
But when wild waves wash o'er the storm swept deck
And your gallant ship is a battered wreck,
Ah, that is the time when it's well worth while
To look in the face of defeat with a smile!

It's easy to laugh when the battle's fought
And you know that the victory's won;
Yes, easy to laugh when the prize you sought
Is yours when the race is run;
But here's to the man who can laugh when the blast
Of adversity blows; he will conquer at last,
For the hardest man in the world to beat
Is the man who can laugh in the face of defeat.
— EMIL CARL AURIN[36]

Life can get pretty tense at times and can seem almost like a tightrope, as if you are doing a balancing act, about to fall into a pit.

This is the time to make a conscious effort to relax, and go forward, learning to laugh and to let go of tensions.

> *A well-developed sense of humor is the pole that adds balance to your step as you walk the tightrope of life.*
> —WILLIAM ARTHUR WARD

Life is not a vending machine. We are not able to put money in and choose a certain item by the code number next to it. No, life hands a circumstance to us, and we determine what we do with the serving allotted to us. True, some people's attitudes seem to bring on fateful experiences because thoughts are magnets and seem to attract like things. We can have a bearing on our surroundings by our thoughts, but some things happen that have nothing to do with thoughts—it is simply life lived.

> *No man can choose what coming hours may bring*
> *To him of need, of joy, of suffering;*
> *But what his soul shall bring unto each hour*
> *To meet its challenge – this is in his power.*
> —PRISCILLA LEONARD

The choice of attitude in any given situation is for each of us to make. We can rise by our thoughts and conquer or slip into despair by allowing ourselves to do so. The question is, "Will we fit the category of a *little* mind or a *great* mind?" That is the one thing that we all will choose: the attitude of our mind and thoughts. We will either rise or fall by our attitude.

> *Little minds are tamed and subdued by misfortune; but great minds rise above them.*
> —WASHINGTON IRVING (1783-1859)
> American essayist, biographer, and historian

Difficulties are times of revelation. They reveal what is inside a person. It is in the time of trial that strength can be forged into the soul. At the same time, a similar trial that strengthens one can weaken another simply because of the attitude chosen by the one who suffers. Hardships are not to weaken but to strengthen if allowed.

Difficulties strengthen the mind, as labor does the body.
—SENECA (4 BC-AD 65)

Full name: Lucius Annateus Seneca. Famous Roman
Philosopher and playwright

Booker T. Washington showed to the world that anyone can make it if he desires to do so bad enough. Not much was known of his father, but he was from birth the property of James Burroughs. He rose from slavery and illiteracy to become the foremost educator and leader of the black community of his time. The attitude that caused him to rise to a place of respected prominence is reflected in the quotation below:

No race can prosper till it learns that there is as much dignity in till-ing a field as in writing a poem.
—BOOKER T. WASHINGTON (1856-1915)

College president, educator, speaker

In 1856, Booker was born in a one-room cabin on a plantation in Virginia. Six years later, in 1862 President Abraham Lincoln issued the Emancipation Proclamation. With the war ending and the Confederacy sinking in defeat, the shattered South was unable to cope with the schooling of its former slaves. These circumstances altered Washington's life completely.

When he was nine years old, Booker's mother and her children migrated, most of the way on foot, to Malden, West Virginia. After arriving there Booker worked in coal mines, sawed wood, and plowed fields. At night he attended an elementary school for black children.

He heard two miners talk about a black school at Hampton, Virginia, so he set out at the age of seventeen, with a few dollars in his pocket, to cover the five hundred miles to the institution. To pay his board he worked as a janitor and waiter; and to fit himself for a trade he studied bricklaying. Soon after graduation he was given a place on the faculty.

Down at Tuskegee, Alabama, a white merchant, George Campbell, and his friend, Lewis Adams, a skilled black workman, conceived the idea of a training school for the black race. Through a friend in the state legislature, Campbell secured an appropriation of two thousand dollars. When he wrote to Hampton Institute for a principal, Booker T. Washington was recommended. Arriving at Tuskegee, the eager young principal asked, "Where's the school?"

"There isn't any — yet," he was told. Undismayed, he declared he would build one. In the meantime he obtained permission to use a small black church. Then he went about making friends and inviting young blacks to come to Tuskegee.

A man of lesser vision and determination would have been discouraged at what Washington saw. Most blacks worked for a pittance. Their houses were shacks, their clothing coarse homespun, their food a diet of salt pork and beans. Disease was prevalent.

Professor Washington decided that cultural education without vocational training would be a waste of time. He named the school "Tuskegee Normal and Industrial Institute," and announced that every student would have to work with his or her hands.

The school opened on July 4, 1881. Thirty persons came in, mostly from nearby cotton fields. The roof leaked so badly that on rainy days the pupils held umbrellas over their heads. Later, with five hundred dollars Washington borrowed from friends at Hampton, they bought an old plantation near town and laid the foundation for Porter Hall, their first building.

Booker Washington was forced to meet deep-seated prejudices. "Educate a Negro and he won't work!" was an oft-repeated maxim among Southern white people. Among black free men was the persistent belief that the one purpose of education was to prepare a person to live in leisure without hard work. A delegation of blacks protested against manual labor as a part of the Institute's program. Washington told them, "There is as much dignity in tilling a field as in writing a poem. And it is as important for your girls to know how to set a table and keep a house as it is to read Latin."

In 1901 Booker wrote a bestseller, *Up from Slavery.* He proved that success is not about environment, prejudice, or men's opinions, but it about attitude, determination, and persistence. He arose from poverty to distinction and helped make the world a better place because he believed that he could do so. His dream was bigger than his circumstance.

> *A man is not hurt so much by what happens, as by his opinion of what happens.*
>
> —MICHEL DE MONTAIGNE (1533-1592)
> French essayist and philosopher

Two people walking through the same circumstance can have totally different outcomes simply by what they believe or the attitude with which they approach it. Put John Bunyan in a prison, and you get *Pilgrim's Progress*. He chose to create in his prison instead of cursing it. Take away the hearing of a great musician, and Beethoven delivers to the world some of his finest works. Afflict a boy with asthma until he lies choking in his father's arms, and you have a Theodore Roosevelt. They chose to rise higher than their circumstances and rose to great heights. Their minds were stronger than the things that seemed to bind and cripple them.

> *A weak mind is like a microscope, which magnifies trifling things but cannot receive great ones.*
> — LORD CHESTERFIELD (1694-1773)
> Philip D. Stanhope, English writer, orator, and statesman

Those who choose to rise higher than the circumstances that dictate failure do not have weak minds. They can receive great ideas because they choose not to magnify the thing that will destroy them. Their attitude is an overcoming one that causes them to alter that which surrounds them. When Winston Churchill faced defeat after Dunkirk, and the invasion of England seemed certain, those became the finest days during World War II simply because one man spoke for the defenseless islanders, "We shall defend our island whatever the cost may be; we shall fight on the beaches; we shall fight in the fields; we shall fight in the streets; and we shall fight in the hill. We shall never surrender!" He literally brought hope to the despaired island because of his mind-set and belief.

> *The greatest discovery of my generation is that human beings can alter their lives by altering their attitudes of mind.*
> — WILLIAM JAMES (1842-1910)
> American philosopher. In 1872 he joined the Harvard faculty as lecturer, continuing to teach until 1907

Some people divide the races into two categories: the optimist and the pessimist, while others add a third: the realist. One thing is certain: the pessimist will never do anything that will cause him to rise because he is always complaining and making excuses about what has befallen him. It is best to be an optimist and add a dash of realism to make a bad situation turn out good.

> *The pessimist complains about the wind; the optimist expects it to change; the realist adjusts the sails.*
> —WILLIAM ARTHUR WARD

The people who think rich thoughts that are different than the norm, that race ahead of the crowd and delve into the unknown, are often the ones who are criticized and ridiculed. This is because they dare to break out of the mold, to rise out of the rut, and to bring light and freedom to others; therefore, they become a target for the little minds that have not caught up with them yet.

One such man was Abraham Lincoln. His name is synonymous with freedom. When he became the sixteenth President of the United States in 1861, he felt it was his moral duty to abolish slavery. Although he had many friends who supported him, he also suffered much criticism for doing so. When Lincoln was asked how he dealt with all his critics, he answered, "If I were to try to read, much less to answer, all the attacks made on me, this shop might as well be closed for any other business. I do the very best I know how — the very best I can; and I mean to keep on doing so until the end. If the end brings me out all right, then what is said against me won't matter. If the end brings me out wrong, then ten angels swearing I was right would make no difference."[37]

Abraham Lincoln is also famous for saying, "You are about as happy as you make up your mind to be." He lived this even in the midst of his sorrows, as he was a man who knew many sorrows, but those times were what caused him to be the one whom God chose to free the slaves, as captured in the following reading by Ruth Sanderson:

Seeking a deliverer, the great God in His own purpose passed by the palace, and its silken delights, and He took a little babe in His arms and called to His side His favorite angel, the angel of sorrow.

Stooping He whispered. "O Sorrow, thou well beloved teacher, take thou this child of mine and make him great.

"Take him to yonder cabin in the wilderness; make his home a poor man's home; plant his narrow path thick with thorns; cut his little feet with sharp rocks as he climbs the hill of difficulty.

"Make each footprint red with his own life blood; load his little back with burdens; give to him days of toil and nights of study and sleeplessness.

"Wrest from his arms whatever he loves; make his heart, through sorrow, as sensitive to the sigh of a slave as a thread of silk in a window is

sensitive to the slightest wind that blows; and when you have digged lines of pain in his cheek and made his face more marred than the face of any man of his time, bring him back to me, and with him I will free 4,000,000 slaves."

That is how God made Abraham Lincoln.[38]

SUCCESS STORY:
HAROLD RUSSELL

Russell, a paratrooper in World War II, lost both his hands in an accident in a training camp. During the first few weeks after this tragedy, he was filled with agony and despair. He became frightened at the thought of going through life with only hooks where his hands should have been. He dreaded going out into the real world and facing the people.

One day Charley McGonegal, who had lost his own hands in World War I, visited Russell in the hospital. His purpose was to help Russell see that the first obstacle he had to overcome was his attitude toward his handicap. The major told him that he was not crippled, just handicapped. Soon after that, Russell went to the hospital library and looked up the two words. *Crippled* meant "disabled, incapable of proper or effective action." *Handicapped* meant "any disadvantage or hindrance making success in an undertaking more difficult."

Slowly he made his way back from despair to triumph. He became a successful actor and writer and, because of his fame, went on lecture tours, speaking on the radio, trying to help people to realize that a handicap does not make them worthless.

In his autobiography, he wrote the following:

> *Each of us must find out for himself that his handicaps, his failures and shortcomings must be conquered or else he must perish. . . . My weakness – my handlessness – my sense of inferiority – has turned out to be my greatest strength. I didn't think so at the time it happened and I don't think I'd ever willingly lose my hands, if I had it to do all over again. But having lost them, I feel perhaps I have gained many fine things I might never have had with them. In a purely material sense, I know I am better off than I ever was before. But that is not the important thing. The important thing is that this seeming disaster had brought me a priceless wealth of the spirit that I am sure I could never have possessed otherwise. I have enjoyed a life that has been full and rich and rewarding, a life that has had a meaning and depth it never had before.*

There is no easy formula for happy living. . . But there is one simple thought I should like to pass on . . . because I found it can help prevent much vain regret and self-defeat. It is not what you have lost, but what you have left that counts. *Too many of us squander precious energy, time, and courage dreaming of things that were and never can be again, instead of dedicating ourselves to realities and the heavy tasks of today.*

People frequently marvel at the things I can do with my hooks. Well, perhaps it is marvelous. But the thing I never cease to marvel at is that I was able to meet the challenge of utter disaster and master it. For me, that was and is the all-important fact — that the human soul, beaten down, overwhelmed, faced by complete failure and ruin, can still rise up against unbearable odds and triumph.[39]

Attitude is the line that separates those who make it and those who do not. It is not what happens to us that ruins or embitters us; our attitude determines the difference. Eventually life deals everyone some hard blows; the key is to keep reevaluating what the blows are doing to us. Are we becoming bitter or better, stronger or weaker, defeating ourselves or growing in the trial? We can fly or we can be chained to a treadmill of disappointments. We each hold the key by what attitude we choose to adopt.

SUCCESS NUGGETS:

I thank God for my handicaps, for, through them, I have found myself, my work, and my God. — HELEN KELLER[40]

THE WINDS OF FATE
One ship drives east and another drives west
With the selfsame winds that blow.
'Tis the set of the sails
And not the gales
Which tells us the way to go.

Like the winds of the sea are the ways of fate,
As we voyage alone through life:
'Tis the set of a soul
That decides its goal,
And not the calm or the strife.
— ELLA WHEELER WILCOX[41]

And he alone is great who turns the voice of the wind into a song made sweeter by his own loving.

— KAHIL GIBRAN[42]

5

BE

SELF-DISCIPLINED

"I keep under my body, and bring it into subjection" (I Corinthians 9:27).

Every person has an empire to rule. It is the inner self. The daily decisions that every individual makes will either refine or pollute the empire. Time has a way of revealing the way a person rules; for decisions made concerning the raging war within will eventually be etched upon each face. People do not just evolve into a certain person, but choices help form what they become. Those who rule with determination, resolve, and strength of will always have more control over self; therefore, they will have a more fruitful life.

What we do on some great occasion will probably depend on what we already are; and what we are will be the result of previous years of self-discipline.

—H. P. LIDDON (1829-1890)

English pulpit orator, professor at Oxford (1870-1882). Chancellor in 1886 of St. Paul's Cathedral

It is not the giving in to the whims of self-indulgence that make a person truly happy; it is the mastery over things that cause them to be more self-reliant and progressive. Self-destruction is the soul mate of those who have no control over that which dominates them, and it finally brings them to a feeling of self-hatred. It is not the lack of passions that can destroy a person; instead it is the complete control of passions that bring a feeling of well-being.

> *The happiness of a man in this life does not consist in the absence but in the mastery of his passions.*
> — ALFRED LORD TENNYSON (1809-1802)
> English poet, the most famous of the Victorian age

Proverbs 14:29 says, "He that is slow to wrath is of great understanding: but he that is hasty of spirit exalteth folly."

To be able to rule the spirit is a sign of greatness, as Proverbs 16:32 states: "He that is slow to anger is better than the mighty; and he that ruleth his spirit than he that taketh a city."

Restraint and self-control are almost foreign words to some, but they are still words of power! Those who wish to lead and to control other entities must first learn to control themselves. The excuses often given are simply a giving in to self-indulgence and perpetuating a weakness of will. Power is there for those who long for it, but it must be a burning desire within, in order to attain it.

> *Such power there is in clear-eyed self-restraint.*
> — JAMES RUSSELL LOWELL (1819-1891)
> Outstanding American poet, as well as a literary critic, professor of modern languages at Harvard, and diplomat

James Lowell attended Harvard simply because it was a family tradition for him, but while there he neglected all his work except literature and languages and almost failed to get his degree. In 1840, he graduated from Harvard Law School but was never much interested in the practice of law.

While waiting for legal business, he wrote poetry. His first volume of poems, *A Year's Life*, was published in 1841. He dedicated it to Maria White, the young poet and reformer whom he married. Her influence on Lowell was great. She led him to take a stand against slavery and to support other reform movements.

Lowell was famous for his *Biglow Papers*. The first of these political satires in verse appeared in the Boston *Courier* in 1846. In 1877, President Rutherford B. Hayes appointed him United States Minister to Spain. After three years in Spain, Lowell was transferred to England. His diplomatic duties required little of him except to build up good will for the United States. But his uprightness, learning, humor, and brilliant oratory made him a prominent man in England. It was his wife who became the catalyst that helped him to develop self-discipline and thus to become a happier man.

There are three important areas that need to be addressed so one can work at having authority over himself: the disciplines of the mind, the tongue, and one's time. If the mind comes under the authority of the will, the person will become stronger because the mind will cause the person to do what is right in all areas of his life. And since the things that are spoken literally help to form our destiny, the tongue must be ruled in a steadfast manner. Lastly, anyone who does not discipline his time will be more likely to fail and to stumble through life instead of attaining inward success.

A. **Discipline the mind!**

THINK SUCCESS:

Even if a person does not speak, his actions will tell what he is thinking, for it is the doing that reveals the thinking.

> *The actions of men are the best interpreters of their thoughts.*
> —JOHN LOCKE (1632-1704)
> English physician

> *Thought is the blossom; language the bud; action the fruit behind it.*
> —RALPH WALDO EMERSON

BELIEVE IN THE HEROIC
"Ah!" said Coningsby, "I should like to be a great man!"
The stranger threw at him a scrutinizing glance. His countenance was serious. He said in a voice of almost solemn melody: —
"Nurture your mind with great thoughts. To believe in the heroic makes heroes."
—BENJAMIN DISRALI[43]

Thinking is so powerful that it rules a person! If someone thinks he can do something, look out; it shall be done, but if he believes he can't, then that same belief system will hinder him from doing what he could do if he thought he could do it.

> *Whether you think you can or think you can't, you're right.*
> — HENRY FORD

> *A man to carry on a successful business must have imagination. He must see things as in a vision, a dream of the whole thing.*
> — CHARLES M. SCHWAB

- Henry Ford said: "Anyone who stops learning is old — whether at twenty or eighty. Anyone who keeps learning stays young. The greatest thing in life is to keep your mind young."[44] This is done through self-discipline and continually studying, learning, and keeping an open mind.
- Richard W. Campbell, who achieved a phenomenal record selling life insurance for the Fidelity Mutual Life Insurance Company, said, "In this world, we either discipline ourselves, or we are disciplined by the world."[45] He said that before he became successful nobody could get much lower in spirit and more discouraged than he was. He couldn't pay his bills and was always broke. The tougher things got; the fewer people he called on. He became so ashamed of his reports that he began to pad them with calls he never made. He said he began to cheat himself. One day he drove way out into the country on a lonely road and turned off the ignition. He sat there for three hours. He asked himself, "Why did you do this?" He said, "Campbell, if that's the kind of fellow you are — if you're going to be crooked with yourself, you're going to be crooked with the other fellow. You're doomed to failure! There's only one choice to make, and the choice must be made by you — and now. No other time will do — it's got to be done *now!*" He chose to discipline his mind before he could influence other people.
- Winston Churchill, in an autobiography written in 1930, *My Early Life*, expressed his regret that he did not have university training. Even though he regretted his waste of time, it caused him to write, "But I now pity undergraduates, when I see what frivolous lives many of them lead in the midst of precious, fleeting opportunity. After all, a man's life must be nailed to a cross, either of thought or of action. Without work, there is no play."[46]

Disciplining the mind is the best thing a person can do for himself, because that is the force that rules his life. The theme of Proverbs 23:7, "As he thinketh in his heart, so is he," has been expounded on by many writers. James Allen wrote his famous book, *As a Man Thinketh*, from the basis of this passage.

He wrote, "A man's mind may be likened to a garden, which may be intelligently cultivated or allowed to run wild; but whether cultivated or neglect, it must, and will bring forth. If no useful seeds are put into it, then an abundance of useless weed-seeds will fall therein; and will continue to produce their kind. Just as the gardener cultivates his plot, keeping it free from weeds, and growing the flowers and fruits which he requires, so may a man tend the garden of his mind, weeding out all the wrong, useless, and impure thoughts, and cultivating toward perfection the flowers and fruits of right, useful, and pure thoughts. By pursuing this process, a man sooner or later discovers that he is the master-gardener of his soul, the director of his life."

Disciplining the mind should become one of the most important things we do in life, for in doing do, we help shape our destiny.

> *Destiny is no matter of chance. It is a matter of choice: It is not a thing to be waited for; it is a thing to be achieved.*
> —WILLIAM JENNINGS BRYAN (1860-1925)
> Noted orator and statesman— from 1891-1895 he served in the United States House of Representatives.

B.   Discipline the tongue!

To discipline the tongue is to save one from much regret, the possibility of the loss of friends, and ill will. The tongue can generate much good or much evil as stated in Proverbs 18:21: "Death and life are in the power of the tongue." It is the one thing that can spark a fire from which the heat can be felt around the world. The importance of the tongue must be impressed upon our consciousness. Wise are the people who learn to teach their mouth what to say, as recorded in Proverbs 16:23: "The heart of the wise teacheth his mouth, and addeth learning to his lips."

> *Govern the lips as they were palace doors, the king within: tranquil and fair and courteous be, all words which from that presence win.*
> —SIR EDWIN ARNOLD (1832-1904)[47]
> English author

It is best to leave things unsaid than to say them if they would cause broken friendships, family misunderstandings, or inward agony. A person is judged by what he says and how he says it. Words can be as razors or swords, or they can be gentle and soothing. The tongue is a mighty emperor and, if used correctly, can rule the masses.

Abraham Lincoln knew the power of the tongue and used this to impart a message that would become one of the most famous speeches in the world. The oration spanned only two minutes. Edward Everett was the man who spoke before him, and he spoke two hours. The world does not remember what Edward Everett said, but they do remember Abraham Lincoln's Gettysburg Address.

It was the president's second inauguration. On March 4, 1865, the streets were filled with milling crowds of people, with cavalry patrols and police. The inauguration platform had been built on the east front of the Capitol, where there was a vast sea of people filling the great plaza and flooding into the grounds beyond. As the President appeared and took his place on the platform, the crowd gave a tremendous roar.

Abraham Lincoln had not expected such a great ovation, for he had been hated and bitterly denounced during the past four years, which were filled with great struggle and suffering, with agony and bloodshed. He had taken over the leadership of the country at a time of grave crisis and had given his best efforts to maintaining and preserving the Union.

He had not expected to be re-elected and felt no elation either at the recent victories in the war or in his own unexpected victory at the polls. He saw the hand of God in both these events and was humbly grateful for the chance now given him to complete his great task. He felt no resentments and had no wish for retaliation against those who had cruelly slandered and abused him. He had one goal: to reconcile and to rebuild the Union he had sworn to preserve.

His two-minute speech has been called "the purest gold of human eloquence." He ended it with these words: "With malice toward none; with charity for all; with firmness in the right, as God gives us to see the right, let us strive on to finish the work we are in; to bind up the nation's wounds; to care for him who shall have borne the battle, and for his widow and his orphan — to do all which may achieve and cherish a just and lasting peace among ourselves and with all nations."

It has been recorded by historians that when Abraham Lincoln stepped forward to make his speech, the sun, which had been obscured all day, suddenly burst through the clouds and flooded the scene with brightness. He spoke slowly and clearly, his voice vibrant with emotion.

It was not the length of Abraham Lincoln's words but the message he delivered. The brevity was more effective than a long discourse.

Abraham Lincoln once said, "It is better to remain silent and be thought a fool than to speak out and remove all doubt." These words are found in Proverbs 17:28: "Even a fool, when he holdeth his peace, is counted wise."

Frank Bettger, who became one of the world's greatest salesmen, realized this truth also and reflected this in his writings, "Overtalking is one of the worst of all social faults."[48]

He acknowledged that he had the problem, and one day one of his best friends took him aside and said, "Frank, I can't ask you a question without your taking fifteen minutes to answer it, when it should only take one sentence!"

Bettger further stated, "But the thing that really shook me awake was the time I was interviewing a busy executive, and he said: 'Come to the point! Never mind all those details.' He didn't care anything about the arithmetic. He wanted the answer. I got to thinking about the sales I had probably lost, the friends I had bored and the time I had lost."[49]

Mencius, the Chinese philosopher, told the story: "Frogs croak day and night, yet men loathe them. But when the cock crows only once, everything under the sky comes into motion. It is important to speak at the proper time, and that is all. What is the good of talking much?"[50]

The truth of saying too much is reflected in the writings of many famous men and women. The story is told of how a young man was sent to Socrates to learn oratory. On being introduced to the philosopher, he talked so incessantly that Socrates asked for double fees. "Why charge me double?" he asked.

"Because I must teach you two sciences: the one how to hold your tongue and the other how to speak. The first science is the more difficult, but aim at proficiency at it, or you will suffer greatly and create trouble without end."[51]

To control and discipline the tongue is one of the first things a successful person must learn to do. This will lead to a feeling of self-respect and respect from others. It is a victory that is worth the fight that it takes to win.

> *There is no finer sensation in life than that which comes with vic-*
> *tory over one's self. It feels good to go fronting into a hard wind, win-*
> *ning against its power; but it feels a thousand times better to go*
> *forward to a goal of inward achievement, brushing aside all your old*
> *internal enemies as you advance.*[52]
>
> — VASH YOUNG (1888-?)
> American author

C. Discipline your time!

Time is one of the greatest gifts to mankind. What is done with this gift depends largely on the individual. To be able to budget time and spend it more wisely is in the same category of budgeting one's money. To lose control of how money is spent is a disaster. It is just as disastrous to lose control over one's time. To feel tense and driven because of a lack of planning and budgeting of time is a modern-day malady.

Arnold Bennett penned one of the greatest discourses on time. He was a low-paid young clerk in a London law office but dreamed of a brilliant and successful writing career. He felt like he had the essential qualities to do this, but he had no time — or so he thought. The more he thought about his dilemma, the more he realized that *time* was his most precious commodity and that he must not waste any of it.

Arnold began to budget his time and worked out a system of self-discipline, permitting no waste of precious time to interfere with his plans. He found that his plan worked. He budgeted his time so that every hour served some useful purpose. Stories and articles that he had written began to be published. Then his first novel was published and his writing began to attract attention.

People would often ask him the question, "Where do you find the time?" This irritated him every time he heard it. He did not find the time; he utilized the same time that everyone else had. It was the way he used his time that made the difference. The more he thought about it, the more he realized he wanted to write a book about the subject, so he did. Following is an excerpt from the book, *How to Live on Twenty-Four Hours a Day:*

> *Time is the inexplicable raw material of everything. With it, all*
> *is possible; without it, nothing. The supply of time is truly a daily*
> *miracle, an affair genuinely astonishing when one examines it.*
> *You wake up in the morning, and lo! your purse is magically filled*

with twenty-four hours of the unmanufactured tissue of the universe of your life! It is yours. It is the most precious of possessions. . . . No one can take it from you. It is unstealable. And no one receives either more or less than you receive. . . . We never shall have any more time. We have, and we have always had, all the time there is.

Arnold Bennett's book made people keenly aware of the value of time and the importance of using leisure time to some advantage instead of just frittering it away. The book was a success. The message of the book is still true and can help anyone learn to budget his time more carefully so he can reach their dreams.

It is essential to plan each day instead of just loafing about doing nothing. There is a time for vacations, but when every day is wasted, some changes need to be made. Victor Hugo, author of the famous *Les Miserables*, wrote the following paragraph and was known to write every day at least one hundred lines of verse or twenty pages of prose:

He who every morning plans the transactions of the day, and follows out that plan, carries a thread that will guide him through the labyrinth of the most busy day. The orderly arrangement of his time is like a ray of light which darts itself through all his occupations. But where no plan is laid, where the disposal of time is surrendered merely to the chance of incidents, all things lie huddled together in one chaos, which admits of neither distribution nor review.
— VICTOR HUGO (1802-1885)
French poet and novelist

Time management is a light that guides the day. Anyone who plans their time will not stumble in the dark but knows where he is going even when well-laid plans are aborted for a short time. It is imperative in order to accomplish one's dreams that one be a planner of the precious gift of time.

Dost thou love life? Then do not squander time, for that's the stuff life is made of. If time be of all things most precious, wasting time must be the greatest prodigality; since lost time is never found again and what we call time enough always proves little enough. Let us then be up and doing, and doing to the purpose; so by diligence shall we do more with less perplexity.
— BENJAMIN FRANKLIN (1706-1790)

D. Discipline Self

A person who can discipline himself will not need to be disciplined by others. Self-disciplined people have the advantage over those who are ruled by their appetites, lusts, and weaknesses. To be able to take authority over self and the raging passions that would bring defeat is to conquer. It is imperative for one to discipline his own spirit as so wisely stated in Proverbs 25:28: "He that hath no rule over his own spirit is like a city that is broken down, and without walls." To not discipline self is to leave oneself open to dangerous consequences.

Let not self rule, but rule self, so the better person can emerge. In so doing you will protect your name. "A good name is rather to be chosen than great riches, and loving favour rather than silver and gold" (Proverbs 22:1).

Seek to live in such a way that your name is protected. Give no fodder to the greedy media that would love to uncover hidden dirt. Life is like a recording studio. You are the artist, and what you do or say is recorded and somebody will remember. People can lie about you, but lies are flimsy and cannot stand against truth.

> *I hope I shall always possess firmness and virtue enough to maintain what I consider the most enviable of all titles, the character of an "honest man."*
> —GEORGE WASHINGTON[53]

A good name, a glow of satisfaction, fulfillment: these should be what spur people to greater things, not just attaining money. Success isn't so much about money, although it is good to have enough to live comfortably and to be able to give to God's kingdom. Making money does not mean success.

William James once wrote: "The cash interpretation put upon the word 'success' is our national disease."[54]

True success is the light within, the delight that comes from reaching a goal or of accomplishing something worthwhile.

SUCCESS STORY:

THOMAS EDISON

Thomas Edison did not give up when his first efforts to find an effective filament for the carbon incandescent lamp failed. He did countless experiments with countless kinds of materials, and as each failed, he would toss it out the window. The pile reached to the second story of his house. Then he sent men to China, Japan, South America, Asia, Jamaica, Ceylon, and Burma in search of fibers and grasses to be tested in his laboratory. One weary day on October 21, 1879—after thirteen months of repeated failures—he succeeded in his search for a filament that would stand the stress of electric current. This was how it happened:

Casually picking up a bit of lampblack, he mixed it with tar and rolled it into a thin thread. Then the thought occurred: Why not try a carbonized cotton fiber? For five hours he worked, but it broke before he could remove the mold. Two spools of thread were used up. At last a perfect string emerged—only to be ruined when trying to place it in a glass tube. Edison refused to admit defeat. He continued without sleep for two days and nights. Finally, he managed to slip one of the carbonized threads into a vacuum-sealed bulb. And he turned on the current. "The sight we had so long desired to see finally met our eyes."

The greatest test of a man's character is how he takes charge of his own life. Harry E. Fosdick once wrote, "No man need stay the way he is." It was Edison's persistence and self-discipline amidst such discouraging odds that has given the world the wonderful electric light. He took charge of his life in spite of his handicaps.

If there is such a thing as luck, then I must be the most unlucky fellow in the world. I've never once made a lucky strike in all my life. When I get after something that I need, I start finding everything in the world that I don't need. I find ninety-nine things that I don't need, and then comes number one hundred, and that—at the very last—turns out to be just what I had been looking for.

—THOMAS ALVA EDISON (1847-1931)[55]

SUCCESS NUGGETS:

No man can produce great things who is not thoroughly sincere in dealing with himself.
—JAMES RUSSELL LOWELL[56]

Self-Control — *Have I the ability to hold the master of myself under trying circumstances? Have I the ability to be pleasant and considerate even though others are unfair and irritable?*
—THE PYTHAGOREAN[57]

TO CONQUER SELF

'Tis a good thing sometimes to be alone,
Sit calmly down, search every secret place.
Prayerfully uproot the baneful seeds there sown,
Pluck out the weeds ere the full crop is grown,
Gird up the loins afresh to run the race,
Foster all noble thoughts, cast out the base,
Thrust forth the bad, and make the good thine own.
Who has this courage thus to look within,
Keep faithful watch and ward with inner eyes;
The foe may harass, but can ne'er surprise,
Or over him ignoble conquest win.
Oh, doubt it not, if thou wouldst wear the crown,
Self, baser self, must first be trampled down.

—JOHN ASKHAM[58]

The virtue of all achievement is victory over oneself. Those who know this victory can never know defeat.

—A. J. CRONIN[59]

Taken from "The Old Soldier's Prayer"

"And after all these things are his, add, I pray, enough of a sense of humor, so that he may always be serious, yet never take himself too seriously. Give him humility, so that he may always remember the simplicity of true greatness, the open mind of true wisdom and the meekness of true strength.

"Then I, his father, will dare to whisper, 'I have not lived in vain'."

—GENERAL DOUGLAS A. MACARTHUR[60]

6
BE
CONFIDENT

"In the fear of the LORD is strong confidence" (Proverbs 14:26).

There is confidence when God is involved. "For with God nothing shall be impossible," the angel told Mary, the mother of Jesus (Luke 1:37). Then Jesus, after beginning His ministry, spoke this truth in Mark 10:27, "With God all things are possible."

Confidence is assurance, belief, and certainty. It is to not doubt but to trust and not fear.

Charles F. Kettering, the noted scientist and inventor, believed the easiest way to overcome defeat was to ignore completely the possibility of failure. In an address delivered at Denison University, Granville, Ohio, he told how he had once given a tough assignment to a young research worker at the General Motors laboratory. Just to see how he would react to a difficult problem, Mr. Kettering forbade him to examine notes on the subject that were filed in the library. These notes were written by expert research men and contained statistics to prove that the assignment was impossible. The young research worker did not know this, of course, so he went to work with confidence that he would succeed.

He did succeed. He didn't know that it couldn't be done, so he did it.[61]

Be Confident

> *They can conquer who believe they can.*
> — VIRGIL (70-19 BC)
> Roman poet

A mother believed this, had confidence in her son, and transferred it to him — Enrico Caruso (1873-1921).

As a boy, he worked long hours in a factory in Naples, but he yearned to be a singer. When he was ten years old, he took his first voice lesson. His teacher told him: "You can't sing. You haven't any voice at all. Your voice sounds like the wind in the shutters."

The boy's mother, however, had visions of greatness for her son. She believed that he had a talent to sing. She was very poor and had nineteen other children [Enrico was the nineteenth child]. Putting her arms around him, she encouragingly said, "My boy, I am going to make every sacrifice to pay for your voice lessons." Her confidence in him and constant encouragement paid off![62]

He became an Italian operatic tenor and had one of the most brilliant voices in the history of music. He made his major debut at Caserta, Italy, in 1895. Three years later, he achieved international fame as creator of the leading tenor role at the world premiere of *Fedora*. After five years of engagements in St. Petersburg, Buenos Aires, Rome, London, and other cities, Caruso began his association with the Metropolitan Opera Company in New York City. His success was almost unparalleled. Caruso mastered at least sixty-seven operatic roles, and his repertoire included about five hundred songs.

Belief that one can do something is the first step to victory. John Stuart Mill wrote: "One person with a belief is equal to a force of ninety-nine who only have interest."[63]

Accomplishments and dreams are realized because somebody believed that he could do it. Confidence is a conviction that it will happen sooner or later. One such young girl believed that she could change her world and did so. The following brief quote summarizes why:

> *Believe in yourself, learn, and never stop wanting to build a better world.*
> — MARY MCLEOD BETHUNE (1875-1955)

Mary Bethune was born on July 10, 1875, the sixteenth child, to parents who had been slaves before her birth but now owned a small plot of land on which they had built the family's cabin. As a young child, Mary wanted to learn to read, but there were no schools open to black children. When Mary turned eleven, however, her dream came true when a mission school opened five miles from her home in Mayesville, South Carolina. The young black teacher from the North sought pupils, and Mary accepted immediately.

She went on to higher education, graduated from Moody Bible Institute in Chicago in 1895, and started a Sunday school in Augusta, Georgia. In 1899, she and her husband, Albertus Bethune, moved to Florida with their infant son, Albert. Mary had heard that a new railroad was being built there, and she knew that there were no schools for African-Americans in that area. In 1904, with only $1.50 saved, she opened the Daytona Normal and Industrial Institute. The private school operated in a rundown four-room cottage that Mary rented. Supplies included boxes used as desks, broken pencils, elderberry ink, and other useful items found at the city dump. There were five girl students aged eight to twelve, and they paid fifty cents per week tuition. The school's motto was "Enter to learn, depart to serve."

Mary had a strong faith and good business sense. Her speaking abilities enabled her to raise money from many sources. In less than two years, she had rebuilt the school and bought the land it sat on. The school's enrollment climbed to 250 students. In 1923, the school merged with the all-male Cookman Institute and later was renamed Bethune-Cookman College. The college, which awarded its first Bachelor of Science degrees in elementary education in 1943, is still prospering today.

She not only was an educator, but she promoted civil rights at the national level. In 1935, she co-founded the National Council of Negro Women, which helped expand public housing and Social Security and welfare programs, and fought against discrimination. The following year, she became national advisor on minority affairs to President Franklin D. Roosevelt. During a speech she made, "A Century of Progress of Negro Women," at the Chicago Women's Federation on June 3, 1933, she made this statement: "The true worth of a race must be measured by the character of its womanhood."

She died on May 18, 1955. In her will, she left the following message for all children, especially for African-American children: "Believe in yourself, learn, and never stop wanting to build a better world."

History is filled with those who believed they were right and who proved that they were. One such person was Cyrus Hall Mc-Cormick, who made the invention of the reaper a success. His biographer said of him: "Confidence of ultimate success after every defeat, and the will to fight on to the last ditch, are two reasons why McCormick outdistanced all his competitors."[64]

SUCCESS STORY:
CYRUS HALL MCCORMICK (1809-1884)

McCormick's father was a mechanical genius and invented many farm devices, but he had become the laughingstock of the community on account of his failure to make a grain-cutting device operate successfully. In spite of the discouragements of his father and the ridicule of the neighbors, young McCormick was determined to succeed. He took up the old machine and, after years of experimentation and failure, in 1831 finally succeeded in constructing a reaper that would cut grain. He patented an improved model in 1834.

But even then jealous opposition prevented it from being used, and it was only after years of labor to introduce it and his personal guarantee to each purchaser that it would harvest the crop, that he succeeded in making sales. After long years of waiting, he arranged with a firm in Cincinnati to manufacture one hundred machines, and the famous McCormick reaper was born.

At the age of thirty-eight, with sixty dollars in his pocket, McCormick went to Chicago. There, he set up his own factory to manufacture reapers. Through years of court action and by purchasing others' patent rights, he established the superiority of his machines and made his company the leader. In 1902, the McCormick holdings were merged into the present International Harvester Company.

In spite of his opponents, McCormick believed in what he was doing and believed that the machine his father had invented was worth the fight. The summation of his biographer bears repeating: "Confidence of ultimate success after every defeat, and the will to fight on to the last ditch, are two reasons why McCormick outdistanced all his competitors."[65]

McCormick had the confidence to fight until he achieved victory. Confidence is an attitude that can help win over any negative situation. It is a belief in something in spite of jeers, fears, or tears.

Confidence is stronger than the mightiest force of opposition. It acts as an army tank rolling over enemy territory with deadly bullets flying in every direction. Nothing can stop confidence! It just keeps going forward in the face of all adversity because it knows it will attain and win.

SUCCESS NUGGETS:

> *Quiet minds cannot be perplexed or frightened, but go on in fortune or misfortune at their own private pace, like a clock during a thunderstorm.*
> — ROBERT LOUIS STEVENSON[66]

> *We shall steer safely through every storm, so long as our heart is right, our intention fervent, our courage steadfast, and our trust fixed on God. If at times we somewhat stunned by the tempest, never fear. Let us take breath, and go on afresh.*
> — FRANCIS DE SALES[67]

> *Being confident of this very thing, that he which hath begun a good work in you will perform it until the day of Jesus Christ.*
> — PHILIPPIANS 1:6

RECIPE FOR SUCCESS
Bite off more than you can chew,
Then chew it.
Plan more than you can do,
Then do it.
Point your arrow at a star,
Take your aim, and there you are.

Arrange more time than you can spare,
Then spare it.
Take on more than you can bear,
Then bear it.
Plan your castle in the air,
Then build a ship to take you there.[68]

7
LIVE LIFE
TO THE FULLEST!

"I am come that they might have life, and that they might have it more abundantly" (John 10:10).

Jesus came so that His children could live an abundant life in Him! It is His will that they walk in His blessings. Today is the best day of your life. Tomorrow may never come and yesterday is history; only today remains. Treat it with respect and live it to the fullest. Let everything you do be done with your style and careful consideration. How should this day be spent? The answer to this question is answered well by Emerson.

> *One of the illusions of life is that the present hour is not the critical, decisive hour. Write it on your heart that every day is the best day of the year. He only is rich who owns the day, and no one owns the day who allows it to be invaded with worry, fret, and anxiety.*
> — RALPH WALDO EMERSON (1803-1882)
> American poet, essayist, and philosopher

To be bothered and fearful is to waste the hour, for fretting and fearfulness are robbers of valuable time. Savor each moment and let it be laced with promise and hope. Think creatively with a mind that is free from clutter and worry. There is no time like now to do what you have always wanted to do. As President Roosevelt said, "Don't fritter away your time."

> *Get action, do things; be sane; don't fritter away your time; create, act, take a place wherever you are and be somebody; get action.*
> — THEODORE ROOSEVELT (1858-1919)[69]

The cry is to wake up! Live the way the Creator intended His creation to live. Why live in mundane boxes when one can break out and reach higher? Where is the excitement that comes with creating something of value and worth? Where did the wonder of life disappear? Has the glow faded and have dreams become tarnished? Are you excitedly awake to the possibilities that surround you?

> *Compared to what we ought to be, we are only half awake. We are making use of only a small part of our physical and mental resources. Stating the thing broadly, the human individual thus lives far within his limits. He possesses powers of various sorts which he habitually fails to use.*
> — WILLIAM JAMES

The joy of life and enthusiasm for the day are there for the asking. One chooses whether or not life becomes dull, without purpose, and full of boredom. Every person is a steward over each new day that he is privileged to live, and what he chooses to do with that day is his prerogative. To be able to *make the most of all that comes and the least of all that goes* is the advice of a survivor depicted in the following poem:

THE MOST WITH THE LEAST
I saw him sitting in his door, trembling as old men do;
His house was old, his barn was old, and yet his eyes seemed
  new.
His eyes had seen three times my years, and kept a twinkle
  still.
Though they had looked at birth and death and three graves
  up a hill.
"I will sit with you," I said, "and you will make me wise:
Tell me how you have kept the joy still burning in your eyes."
Then, like an old-time orator, impressively he arose,
"I make the most of all that comes, and the least of all that goes."

The jingling rhythm of his words echoed as old songs do;
Yet this had kept his eyes alight till he was ninety-two.
—SUNSHINE MAGAZINE

LIVE EACH DAY AS A NEW DAY:

Begin at once to live, and count each separate day as a separate life.
—SENECA THE YOUNGER (5 BC-AD 65)

To count each separate day as a separate life is a concept that eludes many people. The day-after-day living becomes a blurred succession of days put together by the calendar. It takes enlightenment to live fully and to count each day as a gift to be well lived.

It is not enough to live a day and have it go wrong, but lessons learned in that particular day should give insight on how *not* to live a day. Repeat of the same mistakes is a crime against self. *Live and learn* should be the motto of those who desire to live a life that is bursting with purpose and excitement.

Tomorrow is the most important thing in life . . . comes into us at midnight very clean. It's perfect when it arrives and puts itself in our hands. It hopes we've learned something from yesterday.
—JOHN WAYNE (1907-1979)
American actor

To carry failure into each new day is a loathsome thing. Leave failure where it was in the yesterday and take the opportunity to begin all over again. As the glorious morning sun awakens a sleepy world, let it also awaken within you new hope and motivation for better things to come.

Say to yourself these words: "This is a new day. I will not let yesterday's failures darken this day. I choose to live in hope and triumph. I will work toward my goals and accomplish even it takes longer than expected."

Don't let yesterday's blunders or failures darken today's sunlit opportunities. Start your life new with the starting of every hour.
—AUTHOR UNKNOWN

The words *if only* do not belong in the vocabulary of a winner. Yes, learn from mistakes, but to agonize to the point of depression and stagnation is mental suicide. The past is over, but there is a great future awaiting those who pick up and go forward, putting failures under their feet—walking on top of them instead of being buried under them.

> *To be happy, drop the words* if only *and substitute instead the words* next time.
> —SMILEY BLANTON (1882-1966)
> American physician

Each day must be lived with hope for something better. Optimism and anticipation should color each life. To anticipate the possibilities that everyone is surrounded with should be the aspiration of all mankind. It is hope that causes the wounded to press on; hope keeps dreams alive.

Years ago, Dr. Park Tucker was a chaplain of the federal penitentiary in Atlanta, Georgia. He told of walking down the street in a certain city, feeling low and depressed and worried about life in general. As he walked along, he lifted his eyes for a moment to the window of a funeral home across the street. He blinked his eyes a couple of times, wondering whether his eyes were deceiving him.

Sure enough, he saw in the window of that funeral home these words: "Why walk around half-dead? We can buy you for $69.50. P.S. We also give green stamps."

Dr. Tucker said the humor of it was good medicine for his soul. Many people are walking around half-dead because worry has built a mountain of problems over which there is no path, and they have surrendered to fate.[70]

> *Of all the forces that make for a better world, none is so indispensable, none so powerful as hope. Without hope men are only half alive. With hope they dream and think and work.*
> —CHARLES SAWYER (1887-1979)
> Former government official, lawyer, ambassador to Belgium and
> minister to Luxembourg (1944-45), Secretary of Commerce (1948-53)

To choose one's attitude about life is there for each of us to do. We can look upon the new day with wonder or view it with distaste. Life can be lived as an adventure, taking risks, exploring new trails, or can be enclosed in safe boredom. It is a choice: to go near the ocean's edge or to stay at a safe distance, as depicted in Thoreau's words.

My life is like a stroll upon the beach,
As near to the ocean's edge as I can go.
— HENRY DAVID THOREAU (1817-1862)
American writer and philosopher

Living life to the fullest involves people. Abundant life consists of how one chooses to approach his work and what kind of relationships he has. If he does not have something exciting to live for, if his job is a drag, and if he has not found someone to love, he will probably walk with a dragging step and sagging shoulders as if he were carrying a burden.

John Burroughs, the schoolteacher turned naturalist, bears this out in the following paragraph: "Few persons realize how much of their happiness is dependent upon their work, upon the fact that they are kept busy and not left to feed upon themselves. Happiness comes most to persons who seek her least, and think least about it. It is not an object to be sought; it is a state to be induced. It must follow and not lead. It must overtake you, and not you overtake it. . . . Blessed is the man who has some congenial work, some occupation in which he can put his heart, and which affords a complete outlet to all the forces there are in him."

One can live magnificently in this world, if one knows how to work and
how to love, to work for the person one loves and to love one's work.
— LEO TOLSTOY (1828-1910)

To live magnificently is a dream to many, but it can be obtained. To live magnificently is to have a *magnificent obsession,* a tale penned by author Lloyd Douglas in which he relates how a playboy became a respected doctor as his magnificent obsession with medicine became a metaphor for his path to redemption.

Not many people learn how to live magnificently, but it is worth the trip of trying to do so. To erase just an existence and replace it with the excitement of true life is attainable but is not always an easy accomplishment. It matters how badly someone wants it. People choose to live or exist.

To live is the rarest thing in the world. Most people exist, that is all.
— OSCAR WILDE (1854-1900)
Irish dramatist, poet, and wit

"Time and tide for no man wait."
Do it, ere, it is too late.
Seize Time's forelock, do it now;
Hold the locks upon his brow.
When the duty has been done,
You may spell "now" w-o-n.
"Now" spelled backwards means success,
Spelling forward means not less.
Now means now! O list! begin it!
"After a while" or "In a minute"
May be just a bit too late —
　　　　— FLORENCE WELTY MERRELL

To live or to exist is the choice each person makes. Fear can keep people from getting their feet wet in the advancing ocean tide of life. It can stifle the life out of something that was meant to be exciting and alive. To live in a rut simply because of habit or boredom is a crime invoked upon oneself. Life is too short to live in a box of lackluster living. There are adventures waiting to happen, experiences longing to be experienced. Determine today to wake up to life and to enjoy the moment: *seize the day!*

SUCCESS STORY:
HELEN KELLER

In Helen Keller's biography, she describes her reaction to life in three different instances of trips she had taken. It is evident that she lived life to the fullest in spite of the amazing fact that she was deaf and blind.

May 1888, these were her feelings about a trip taken when she was eight years old:

> *In the autumn I returned to my Southern home with a heart of joyous memories. As I recall that visit North, I am filled with wonder at the richness and variety of the experiences that cluster about it. It seems to have been the beginning of everything. The treasures of a new, beautiful world were laid at my feet, and I took in pleasure and information at every turn. I lived myself into all things. I was never still a moment; my life was as full of motion as those little insects that crowd a whole existence into one brief day.*

She expressed living life to the fullest — *I lived myself into all things.*

March 1893, after a visit to Niagara:

It is difficult to describe my emotions when I stood on the point which overhangs the American Falls and felt the air vibrate and the earth tremble.

It seems strange to many people that I should be impressed by the wonders and beauties of Niagara. They are always asking: "What does this beauty or that music mean to you? You cannot see the waves rolling up the beach or hear their roar. What do they mean to you?" In the most evident sense they mean everything. I cannot fathom or define their meaning any more than I can fathom or define love or religion or goodness.

She was *impressed by the wonders and beauties,* and was able to sense, to feel, to experience with her whole being, without her eyes.

Summer 1893, after a visit to the World's Fair with Dr. Alexander Graham Bell:

I recall with unmixed delight those days when a thousand childish fancies became beautiful realities. Every day in imagination I made a trip round the world, and I saw many wonders from the uttermost parts of the earth — marvels of invention, treasuries of industry and skill and all the activities of human life actually passed under my finger tips.

Mr. Higinbotham, President of the World's Fair, kindly gave me permission to touch the exhibits, and with an eagerness as insatiable as that with which Pizarro seized the treasures of Peru, I took in the glories of the Fair with my fingers. It was a sort of tangible kaleidoscope, this white city of the West. Everything fascinated me, especially the French bronzes. They were so lifelike, I thought they were angel visions which the artist had caught and bound in earthly forms.[71]

Everything fascinated me! This is the way to live life to the fullest. Stay alive, be interested; do not become bored with living.

SUCCESS NUGGETS:

THE SALUTATION OF THE DAWN
Listen to the exhortation of the dawn!
Look to this Day!
For it is life, the very life of life.

In its brief course lie all the
Verities and realities of your existence:
    The bliss of growth,
    The glory of action,
    The splendor of beauty,
For Yesterday is but a dream,
And tomorrow is only a Vision:
But today well lived makes
Every yesterday a dream of happiness,
And every tomorrow a vision of hope!
Look well therefore to this day!
Such is the salutation of the dawn![72]

One of the most tragic things I know about human nature is that all of us tend to put off living. We are all dreaming of some magical rose garden over the horizon — instead of enjoying the roses that are blooming outside our windows today.
           — DALE CARNEGIE[73]

One important source of unhappiness is the habit of putting off living to some fictional future date. Men and women are constantly making themselves unhappy because in deferring their lives to the future they lose sight of the present and its golden opportunities for rich living.
           — W. BERAN WOLFE

8

GIVE MORE THAN IS REQUIRED

"God loves a cheerful giver" (II Corinthians 9:7, *New King James Version*).

There has always been a law of the winner: go beyond mere duty—give more than is required. This has been and always will be the thrust that causes one to rise higher than the norm. The runner who keeps running in spite of an injury, the mother who continues even when it is a sacrifice, a president who forges ahead no matter what the opposition, someone who is falsely accused and keeps persisting in what he knows to be right: these all go beyond what is required of them.

Those who win and are successful in life are those who chose to give, even when it is backbreaking work or less than desirable conditions. Winners do not always choose conditions; they conquer them, sometimes even making them. This is the case in the story of Edward H. Harriman.

Harriman was born in 1848, and at age fourteen, he began work as an office boy in a New York brokerage house. Eight years later he bought his own seat on the New York Stock Exchange, and in 1879 married Mary Averell, the daughter of the president of the

Ogdensburg and Lake Champlain Railroad. In 1881 Harriman bought control of the Sodus Bay and Southern Railroad, a short line running south from the shore of Lake Ontario. He improved the line and then set the New York Central and Pennsylvania bidding against each other for it. Pennsy bought it, and Harriman soon went after a larger railroad, the Illinois Central. By 1883 he was on the IC's board of directors. In 1898 Harriman took over the Union Pacific. In 1901 Harriman bought the Southern Pacific and shortly afterward bought the Central Pacific.

Harriman was not one to buy a railroad for a quick profit. He believed that the financial yield would be considerably greater if the railroad's property was improved and its affairs well managed. Harriman established standards for locomotives, cars, bridges, structures, signals, and even such items as paint and stationery. From an office boy, he rose to be a railroad tycoon. Harriman's philosophy is depicted in the following quote:

> *To achieve what the world calls success a man must attend strictly to business and keep a little in advance of the times. The man who reaches the top is the one who is not content with doing what is required of him. He does more.*
>
> —EDWARD H. HARRIMAN (1848-1909)
> Railroad tycoon

Doing more always demands diligence and fortitude. Anyone who wants to lead a pampered life, flitting about doing basically nothing except seeking to have a good time, will eventually lose the very essence of life. Life is not about preserving self and hoarding it, but life is to be spent or given to a worthy cause. This concept is not new. Jesus taught it to His disciples in Luke 9:24: "For whosoever will save his life shall lose it: but whosoever will lose his life for my sake, the same shall save it." The principle is simply to live for a greater cause than self. When lives only for self, it is a miserable existence. The saved life is lost and never accomplishes anything.

> *Life is ours to be spent, not to be saved.*
> —D. H. LAWRENCE (1885-1930)
> English writer

To be truly rich and have a sense of fulfillment, there must always be a giving of self and a spending of one's time. J. B. Priestley once wrote: "To me there is in happiness an element of self-forget-fulness. You lose yourself in something outside yourself when you are happy, just as when you are desperately miserable you are intensely conscious of yourself, are a solid little lump of ego weighing a ton." It is not just an inflated ego that can cause unhappiness but also a low self-esteem that stems from an obsession with one's flaws. This limits an individual and somewhat paralyzes him from moving forward and being successfully happy. It is not the saving of one's self or the obsession with self, but the spending of it on something outside of self that brings true rewards.

In this world it is not what we take up, but what we give up, that makes us rich.
— HENRY WARD BEECHER

"Give, and it shall be given," was first penned in Luke 6:38. The principle still applies, even in this generation. There must first be a giving of something before anything can be received. When you look at someone who has succeeded at something, he will always tell you what it took for him to get there. It was not ease and self-preservation; it was giving beyond what was required.

No person was ever honored for what he received. Honor has been the reward for what he gave."
— CALVIN COOLIDGE (1872-1933)
30th President of the United States

The people who get what they desire will always give more than what is required. It isn't, "How much?" It is, "No matter what it takes, I'm getting it!" This is epitomized in the statement of the editor of the abolitionist paper, *The Liberator*. William Lloyd Garrison (1805-1879) once sold his bed and slept on the floor to buy more newsprint to publish his attacks on slavery. His epitaph cites the courage of honest conviction: "I am in earnest. . . . I will not retreat a single step, and I will be heard."

William did what he could, even if it took going beyond what was required of him to do. His purpose was greater than his sacrifice. When the crowd is crying that it cannot be done and the task looks insurmountable, just do what you can do. You cannot do everything, but you can do something. That is the measure for your life. You cannot compare yourself with others, but try to outdistance your previous performance. Just do what you have to do wherever you are and do not wait for a better opportunity, for as you do so, a better opportunity will appear.

> *There is nothing to be gained by wishing you were someplace else or waiting for a better situation. You see where you are and you do what you can with that.*
>
> —JACOB K. JAVITS (1904-1986)
> US Senator

Your contribution is important, and it is not just for the now. Everything each of us does can touch and will touch someone else; if not now, in some distant future. Longfellow reminded us that if we do something now, maybe in the future that act will affect some poor, discouraged soul:

> *Lives of great men all remind us*
> *We can make our lives sublime*
> *And, departing, leave behind us*
> *Footprints on the sands of time.*
>
> *Footprints, that perhaps another,*
> *Sailing o'er life's solemn main,*
> *A forlorn and shipwrecked brother,*
> *Seeing, shall take heart again.*[74]

If all the inventors, scientists, clergymen, presidents, and other people in the world who enrich other lives decided that they were only one person and could not do much, things would be in a sorry state of affairs. It is essential that everyone do what he can do and not worry that what he is doing matters. It does matter. Everyone working together doing what each can do will bring good into every life that is touched.

> *I am only one; but still I am one.*
> *I cannot do everything,*
> *But still I can do something;*
> *And because I cannot do everything,*
> *I will not refuse to do the something I can do.*
>
> —EDWARD EVERETT HALE (1822-1909)[75]
> American author

Do what you can do! You want to sing but cannot; then do not sing. You want to write but cannot; then do not write. You want to be politician but cannot; then do not run for office. But find out what you *can* do, and do it with all your might!

> *Do not let what you cannot do interfere with what you can do.*
> —JOHN WOODEN (1910- ?)
> American basketball coach

Why be silent when you can speak? Why hang back cowardly when you can advance? Why shrivel when you can grow? Why hide like a fox in a den when you can go forth conquering? Why stagnate when fresh ideas are there to grasp? Why be overwhelmed when victory is for the taking?

> *He who is silent is forgotten; . . . he who does not advance falls back; he who stops is overwhelmed, distanced, crushed; he who ceases to grow greater becomes smaller; he who leaves off, give up; the stationary condition is the beginning of the end.*
> —AMIEL (1821-1881)
> Swiss poet and philosopher, professor at Geneva Academy

If a person can do more than what he is doing, he needs to be prodded, for it is never good to be less than what one can be. God desires for His children to become what He created them to be. The stretching, the reaching, and the going beyond should rule the consciousness of every person.

> *It is right to be contented with what we have, never with what we are.*
> —SIR JAMES MACKINTOSH (1765-1832)
> Scottish statesman and historian

The important thing is for every individual to take stock of his or her own qualities, talents, aptitude, and gifts and then work toward doing something that would enhance those natural abilities. The moment is now, not in some distant future. If everyone waits for that magic moment, it rarely appears. Just plunge in, and go for it with gusto and zest!

> *The question for each man to settle is not what he would do if he had the means, time, influence, and educational advantages; the question is, What will he do with the things he has? The moment a young man. . . resolutely looks his conditions in the face, and resolves to chance them, he lays the cornerstone of a solid and honorable success.*
> —HAMILTON WRIGHT MABIE (1845-1960)
> Lawyer, editor, and author

Give More Than is Required

There have been some who have thrown their energy into their lives' dreams and have been successful; then tragedy overtook them. So what do they do? They have two choices: give up, exist, and even become bitter, or work at finding success in another area that would bring them fulfillment. People do not choose tragedies or disasters, but sometimes they come.

EXAMPLE OF THIS:

A member of the Olympic ice-skating team of 1924, Valentine Bialis, was acclaimed the fastest man on skates. Everywhere he was idolized and honored as king of the ice. Eight years later, as he was preparing to take top honors as ice-skating champion of the world, Valentine Bialis was driving home one dark, drizzly night. The road and his windshield were slowly coating with ice.

Suddenly he heard the screech of a train whistle. He jammed on his brakes and skidded—right into the path of an engine. He was rushed to the hospital seriously injured. He came out of the hospital minus a leg. Gone were his hopes of a championship. He tried to make a comeback skating with one wooden leg, but it was impossible.

Some time later, however, Bialis appeared in the headline of the paper in a small mid-western town. He had won a local tennis tournament. He had failed, through cruel fate, to win a skating championship, but did what he could do and continued to compete in another sport and became tennis champ in a small town. All was not lost, because he refused to give up!

It is the fiber or steel inside a person that is able to refuse to give in to misfortune. To be able to find a new life and to put away the one that brought joy and fulfillment, then to pursue another profession demand sheer willpower and determination. It takes spirit and courage to go forward when a situation dictates otherwise.

> *A man in earnest finds means, or, if he cannot find, creates them. A vigorous purpose makes much out of little, breathes power into weak instruments, disarms difficulties, and even turns them into assistances. Every condition has means of progress, if we have spirit enough to use them.*
>
> —WILLIAM ELLERY CHANNING (1780-1842)
> American author

90

There is no one who can put the will to go forward inside the victim of loss or failure. People can encourage, books can be read, others can coach and give inspiring speeches, but the fire must ignite within the one who has suffered losses in order for him to be able to have the ability to go beyond the hardship and do what he can do with what is left.

> *Always bear in mind that your own resolution to succeed is more important than any other one thing.*
> — ABRAHAM LINCOLN

Whatever it is you want bad enough, be willing to give more than what is demanded of you. Give when others tell you to slow down. Give when others sit and complain of the conditions. Give when everything dictates to you to retreat; push forward anyhow. Do not let the circumstances dictate to you or the difficulties of the race intimidate you, but push forward with all your might and you will win!

> *Be not content with doing your duty. . . . Do more. It is the horse that finishes a neck ahead that wins the race.*
> — ANDREW CARNEGIE (1835-1919)
> Scottish-born American industrialist and philanthropist

SUCCESS STORY:
ANDREW CARNEGIE

Andrew Carnegie was not content with his life. He had five years' schooling in Dumferline, Scotland, where his father wove damask linens in a home shop. In 1848, when Carnegie was thirteen, his family moved to the United States. The father was forty-three at the time of emigration, the mother ten years younger. For an immigrant, the father was too old to start anew, and he drifted helplessly, first finding work as an operative in a cotton mill. It was hard, and he returned to his home hand loom, peddling his wares from door to door.

Andrew went to work in the cotton mill as a bobbin boy at $1.20 a week. The only other formal learning Andrew had was six months in night school (where he was taught double-entry bookkeeping) and some private French lessons. Yet Andrew Carnegie eventually became a highly educated man. He read and learned Shakespeare and poetry, was versed in the classics, and began to collect prints and sculpture and to buy books. Some of his earliest benefactions were the establishment of public libraries and the Carnegie Institute, to include a library, art gallery, music hall, and a museum of natural history, in Pittsburgh.

Because of his father's failure and because of his deep devotion to a mother who kept the little family together in its early years of struggle, Carnegie had a fierce desire to succeed. He acquired skills as he went along and impressed those he worked for with his resourcefulness. He became a telegraph messenger boy; at fifteen a telegraph operator; and at eighteen, the confidential clerk of Thomas A. Scott, the superintendent of the western division of the Pennsylvania Railroad, at that time in the process of building its line across the Alleghenies. Carnegie was making $40 a month (Scott was getting $125) and was the head of the household. He purchased a home for his mother and father (the price was $700, the down payment $100); he saved money; at twenty, he made his first investment— he bought ten shares of Adams Express Company. When he was twenty-one, in 1856, he was already an entrepreneur. He had met T. T. Woodruff, the inventor of the sleeping car, and had persuaded Scott, now the general superintendent of the Pennsylvania, to buy two sleeping cars; Woodruff had offered Carnegie a one-third share in his company. Carnegie went to one of the local banks to finance his first payment. He received a little more than $200 on his personal note; it was the first of many similar transactions that marked the early years of his climb.

Carnegie's young manhood was spent with the railroad industry. In 1859, Scott, his mentor and friend, became vice-president of the Pennsylvania Railroad, and Carnegie succeeded him as manager of the western division. In 1861 he went with Scott to Washington: Scott in charge of military transportation for the Department of the Army, Carnegie specifically responsible for the operation of military railways and telegraphs. In 1862, Carnegie returned to the Pennsylvania and remained with it for another three years.

Carnegie went into iron manufacture at the same time only because the development and future of the railroad industry were linked with iron. With others (his brother Tom included) he set up a small wrought-iron company, then another company to make structural shapes, then one to make iron rails, and still another to make locomotives. The most important was the Keystone Bridge Company, formed in 1863, in which Carnegie had a one-fifth share.

In the early 1870s Carnegie made a fateful decision: to concentrate on the manufacture of iron and steel and be master in that. This was the beginning of his success story. On December 17, 1896, *The Iron Age*, the technical periodical of the industry, after watching Carnegie build bridges, organize new businesses, and introduce mass production, reported that the Carnegie leases and other holdings gave his company "a position unequaled by any steel producer in the world."

In his lifetime he gave away $350 million—to fund libraries, museums and art institutes, pure research, education, and college professors.

Nothing can stop a winner! The giving and going beyond always reap great benefits and rewards. The one who presses on, with victory in mind, will eventually come out on top because of the unchangeable reaping and sowing process.

SUCCESS NUGGETS:

It is more blessed to give than to receive.
—ACTS 20:35

Happiness is a sunbeam which may pass through a thousand bosoms without losing a particle of its original ray; nay, when it strikes a kindred heart, like the converged light upon a mirror, it reflects itself with redoubled brightness. It is not perfected till it is shared.
—JANE PORTER[76]

The habit of giving only enhances the desire to give.
—WALT WHITMAN[77]

There is a wonderful, mystical law of nature that the three things we crave most in life—happiness, freedom, and peace of mind—are always attained by giving them to someone else.[78]

9

GAIN KNOWLEDGE

"Wisdom is the principal thing; therefore get wisdom: and with all thy getting get understanding" (Proverbs 4:7).

Knowledge is power! To know is to learn, to do, to go forward; to be enlightened causes the sun to shine in a darkened mind. Knowledge combats confusion; it erases hesitancy and pushes one onward with new purpose. A blind woman who was deaf penned the phrase many years ago: *knowledge is power*. As her handicap imprisoned her and left her with no ability to witness the light of day, her mind could not be chained. It became alive with pulsating thoughts that lifted her spirits to heights of glory as reflected many times in her writings. The wings in her mind and the lifting of her spirit were attained through knowledge. Helen Keller depicts this in the following paragraph:

I have learned many things. . . . One of them is the precious science of patience, which teaches us that we should take our education as we would take a walk in the country, leisurely, our minds hospitably open to impressions of every sort. Such knowledge floods the soul unseen with a soundless tidal wave of deepening thought. 'Knowledge is power.' Rather, knowledge is happiness, because to have knowledge — broad, deep knowledge — is to know true ends from false, and lofty

things from low. To know the thoughts and deeds that have marked man's progress is to feel the great heart-throbs of humanity through the centuries; and if one does not feel in these pulsations a heaven-ward striving, one must indeed be deaf to the harmonies of life.
— HELEN KELLER

The prepared mind is a fertile mind and readies itself to receive what life drops into its carefully tilled furrows of thought. Idleness and loose thoughts become murderers to dreams. When the mind prepares itself, it seems that time and chance appear as if on cue.

Chance favors only the prepared mind.
— LOUIS PASTEUR (1822-1895)
One of the world's greatest scientists

Five things to know:

A. Where you want to go

B. What you want

C. Your stuff

D. Yourself

E. God!

A. Know where you want to go — direction:

Men must be decided on what they will not do, and then they are able to act with vigor on what they ought to do.
— MENCIUS (372-289 BC)
Chinese philosopher

The day is always his who works in it with serenity and great aims.
— RALPH WALDO EMERSON

If you do not know in what direction to go, begin to explore and to ask questions. If you are not able to go to college, do not let that stop you from learning. Thomas Edison, the greatest inventor in history, had only three months of formal schooling, but he changed the lives of millions of people with such inventions as the electric light and phonograph.

He was born the seventh and youngest child of Samuel and Nancy Edison. The great curiosity of the youngster led him to ask questions constantly. "How does a hen hatch chickens?" "What makes birds fly?" "Why does water put out a fire?" His mother had once been a schoolteacher, but even she could not answer some of his questions. If no one answered his questions, he would try to get the answers by experimentation. For example, he noticed that a hen hatched chicks out of eggs by sitting on them. So the boy collected some eggs and sat on them!

Edison's mother had the notion that learning could be fun. She made a game of teaching him — she called it exploring — the exciting world of knowledge. The boy was surprised at first and then delighted. Soon he began to learn so fast that his mother could no longer teach him.

When Thomas was nine years old, his mother bought him a chemistry book by Richard G. Parker, a well-known teacher of the mid-1800s. Edison would not accept as true the statements made in the book. He tested every experiment himself to try to prove the author wrong. Thomas had more than one hundred bottles containing various chemicals. He labeled them all "Poison" to keep his family away from them.

At the age of twelve, he took a job as "news butcher' on the Grand Trunk Railway. He sold newspapers, candy, sandwiches, and peanuts on a train that ran between Port Huron and Detroit. In his spare time, he experimented with chemicals in the baggage car. He even printed a newspaper, the *Weekly Herald,* the first newspaper to be published on a moving train.

However, one of his experiments got him into trouble. One day, a stick of phosphorus burst into flames and set the baggage car on fire. The conductor boxed the ears of Thomas and threw him off the train — chemicals, printing press, and all.

In 1869, Edison went to New York City nearly penniless and persuaded an employer of the Gold Indicator Company, a stock-ticker firm, to let him sleep in the office. Edison spent much of his time studying the stock ticker, a telegraph device the company used to report the price of gold to brokers' offices. The ticker broke down a few days later, and Edison astounded the manager by fixing it after other persons had failed. The manager at once offered him the job of supervisor at $300 a month, a large salary at that time.

Edison's busy mind kept him experimenting on the stock

ticker. He made improvements that interested General Marshall Lefferts, president of the Gold and Stock Telegraph Company. Lefferts sent for Edison and asked him how much he wanted for his various patents on the stock ticker.

Edison decided he might dare ask for $5,000 but would accept $3,000. Hesitating between the two figures, he said, "Well, General, suppose you make me an offer." Lefferts thought for a while and then said: "How would $40,000 strike you?"

For a moment, Edison had trouble getting control of himself, seized the table to steady himself, and said slowly, "I think that will be fair."

With this money he opened his first workshop in Newark, New Jersey. He never ceased to learn, to explore, and to gain knowledge.

B.   Know what you want — purpose:

Firmness of purpose is one of the most necessary sinews of character, and one of the best instruments of success. Without it genius wastes its efforts in a maze of inconsistencies.
— LORD CHESTERFIELD

Purpose is a requirement in attaining what one desires, but it is not enough to have purpose. What matters also is the day-to-day staying power working toward a goal. To give in to dilatory practices and to waver in purpose are a death sentence to attaining success.

The secret of success is constancy to purpose.
— BENJAMIN DISRAELI (1804-1881)

Disraeli was Earl of Beaconsfield and was the only man to be born a Jew who became Prime Minister of Great Britain. He was largely responsible for the 1867 Parliamentary Reform Act and introduced laws to improve slum conditions, to protect the factory worker, and to help the farm laborer who was in economic distress. He also obtained a major interest in the Suez Canal for Great Britain by purchasing a large number of shares. He described himself as a "conservative to preserve all that is good in our constitution, and a radical to remove all that is bad."

Disraeli had a purpose, and he knew what that purpose was. His tenure in office did much to improve the conditions that he considered to be bad. His surroundings did not dictate to him; his purpose did. The ones who know where they are going are the ones who get there. Guesswork causes confusion and leads down numerous paths that lead nowhere. Purpose is the driving force that reaches its destination.

> *One who is never quite sure of anything – who thinks, guesses, or imagines, about the amount or about the distance – who comes somewhere near, but never is quite certain of anything – rarely gets very far in this world. It is the accurate man, the painstaking man who is exact, who attains to the highest success.*
> —O. S. MARDEN

Busyness is not purpose. Purpose is to know what one is working for and then to follow a plan to reach the goal of the purpose. Purpose is not here today and gone tomorrow; it is there in the morning when one awakens and is there when he goes to bed at night. The purpose is an integral part of his very being. It is the guiding force of his life.

> *It is not enough to be busy; so are the ants. The question is: What are we busy about?*
> —HENRY DAVID THOREAU (1817-1862)
> American writer.

Thoreau is remembered for his attacks on the social institutions he considered immoral and for his faith in the religious significance of nature. His writing of *Walden* in 1854, a study of man living in harmony with nature, is chiefly responsible for his literary reputation. He wrote, "The mass of men lead lives of quiet desperation." He appealed to all men to economize, to simplify their lives, and thus to save the time and energy that would allow them "to live deep and suck out all the marrow of life. . . ."

Thoreau came from a family that was neither wealthy nor distinguished. His father sold pencils, and his mother took in boarders. Thoreau graduated from Harvard College in 1837 and soon met writer Ralph Waldo Emerson, who encouraged him to write, gave him useful criticism, and later employed him as a gardener and a handyman.

Thoreau had purpose: to live a full life, to reflect on nature in order to enrich his writings; and to help mankind live richer lives in freedom from slavery. He is remembered today because of his purposeful writings.

In order to reach a goal or destination, one must know where he is headed. Who would shoot a feather in the breeze and expect it to travel one hundred miles? No one would do this, yet this is how some people live their lives. Each day they flounder and shoot with no aim and with no substance. Somehow they just never get to where they are going.

> *Our plans miscarry because they have no aim. When a man does not know what harbor he is making for, no wind is the right wind.*
> —SENECA THE YOUNGER (5 BC-AD 65)

The individuals who are fortunate to know where they are going are blessed. This in itself is an accomplishment. Many who struggle and are confused say, "If I just knew what I was supposed to do, then I'd do it." It is a sad state of affairs when someone is confused about the direction his life is to go.

> *Happy are those whose purpose has found them.*
> — ANONYMOUS

To know that you have a purpose and that you must fulfill that purpose is a great thing. It lifts a load from the mind and clears the thoughts so that one can think more clearly about the purpose at hand. To have purpose is to have joy.

> *This is the true joy in life, the being used for a purpose recognized by yourself as a mighty one; the being thoroughly worn out before you are thrown on the scrapheap; the being a force of Nature instead of a feverish, selfish, little clod of ailments and grievances complaining that the world will not devote itself to making you happy.*
> —GEORGE BERNARD SHAW (1856-1950)

C.   Know your stuff — skill:

Knute Rockne (1888-1931), famous football coach of University of Notre Dame, Indiana, once said, "At Notre Dame, we have a squad of about three hundred lads — both varsity veterans and newcomers. They keep practicing fundamentals, and keep it up, and keep it up, and keep it up, until these various fundamentals become as natural and subconscious as breathing. Then in the game, they don't have to stop and wonder what to do next when the time comes for quick action."[79]

Skill does not come just by wishful thinking; it comes from

constant practice and doing the same thing over and over again. Many performances that seem effortless were not so but were attained by practicing hours and hours until the performer became skilful.

> *Skill to do comes of doing.*
> — RALPH WALDO EMERSON (1803-1882)

Anyone can learn the rules of a trade, a game, or an endeavor, but it takes years to attain the skills to do it well. To know something is not enough; to improve one's skills requires practice and constant doing. Skill cannot be transferred to anyone; it must be attained.

> *A carpenter or a carriage maker can pass on to another the rules of his craft, but he cannot make him skillful.*
> — MENCIUS (371-289 BC)

The most famous artist and sculptor of the Italian Renaissance admitted that his skill came from hard work, as depicted in the following quote:

> *If people knew how hard I have had to work to gain my mastery, it wouldn't seem so wonderful."*
> — MICHELANGELO (1475-1564)[80]

D. Know thyself:

From the ancients came the quote: "Know thyself and become what you are." Each person needs to recognize the nature of his basic personality, what he is best suited for, then submit to it and become the best he was created to be. Everyone has a destiny; once you find it, pursue it with vigor. It is not enough to know what we are, but it is important to understand the possibilities of what we might become.

> *We know what we are, but know not what we may be.*
> — WILLIAM SHAKESPEARE (1564-1616)
> He is considered the greatest dramatist the world has known, as well as the finest poet who has written in the English language.

It is not an easy thing to know who we are and what we are to become; it is easier to read facts, memorize figures, and compute knowledge than it is to understand the feelings, emotions, and destinies of our life.

Gain Knowledge

It's not only the most difficult thing to know one's self, but the most inconvenient.

—Josh Billings (1818-1885)

Pen name for American humorist, Henry Wheeler Shaw

Josh finally found his destiny. He wrote essays rather than stories, and, unlike many humorists of his time, he always kept a kindly tone. Although he was reckless in his early life, he later became a moralist and what they termed, in his day, a "cracker barrel" philosopher. Billings published annually from 1869 to 1880 *Josh Billings' Farmers' Almanacs*. He published his first book, *Josh Billings, His Sayings*, in 1865.

In the reading General Douglas MacArthur wrote, entitled, "An Old Soldier's Prayer," he included one paragraph about this subject. He said, "Build me a son whose wishes will not take the place of deeds; a son who will know Thee . . . and that to know himself is the foundation stone of knowledge."[81]

To know oneself is important for forging ahead, but in order to do so one must also be able to live with oneself. True knowledge of self should include a goal of continuation of bettering self and becoming a person of self-respect with a good conscience, as the poet so ably depicts in the following poem:

MYSELF

I have to live with myself, and so
I want to be fit for myself to know,
I want to be able, as days go by,
Always to look myself straight in the eye;
I don't want to stand, with the setting sun,
And hate myself for things I have done.

I don't want to keep on a closet shelf
A lot of secrets about myself,
And fool myself, as I come and go,
Into thinking that nobody else will know
The kind of a man I really am;
I don't want to dress up myself in sham.

I want to go out with my head erect,
I want to deserve all men's respect;

But here in the struggle for fame and pelf [riches]
I want to be able to like myself.
I don't want to look at myself and know
That I'm bluster and bluff and empty show.

I can never hide myself from me;
I see what others may never see;
I know what others may never know,
I never can fool myself, and so,
Whatever happens, I want to be
Self-respecting and conscience free.[82]

— EDGAR A. GUEST (1881-1959)

An English-born American poet

God allows things to come our way sometimes for us to know what is deep inside us. "All hindrances are tests. They try the reality of our resolutions and the genuineness of our purposes. God Himself knows us; but we do not know ourselves perfectly well, and the tests which come with hindrances bring us revelation of ourselves."[83]

Oh, to see ourselves as God sees us, to ask for mercy and grace for our weaknesses, and to pray as Paul prayed in Galatians 4:19, "Christ be formed in you"! This is the dream to be Christ controlled, to have Him work in us until we feel good about where He is taking us and what He is doing in us. That is growth and progress in our life's walk.

To protect the heart and mind from evil should be the desire of those who wish to be successful, for Proverbs 4:23 states: "Keep thy heart with all diligence; for out of it are the issues of life."

Edgar Guest articulates, simply but lyrically, the desires that people feel but oftentimes are unable to express. He summed up his aspirations for life in the following verse:

I'd like to think when life is done
That I had filled a needed post,
That here and there I'd paid my fare
With more than idle talk and boast;
That I had taken gifts divine,
The breath of life and manhood fine,
And tried to use them now and then
In service for my fellow men.

For people to live in such a way that they can respect themselves is the ultimate of living. To live without a guilty conscience and to know that one is doing the right thing in each circumstance; this acts as armor from outside influences. To know that each decision is made according to justice, fairness, and what is right gives people self-respect. This protects a person.

He that respects himself is safe from others; He wears a coat of mail that none can pierce.

— HENRY WADSWORTH LONGFELLOW

(1807-1887) American poet

If self-respect begins with each individual, then it is imperative that daily inventory be taken of the way *self* acted. To be able to live with one's self, and feel good about it is the ultimate victory. To lie down at night and know that one did their best that day is a great feeling. This nobleness is reflected in the following poem:

BE TRUE
Thou must be true thyself
If thou the truth wouldst teach;
Thy soul must overflow if thou
Another's soul wouldst reach!
It needs the overflow of heart
To give the lips full speech.

Think truly, and thy thoughts
Shall the world's famine feed;
Speak truly, and each word of thine
Shall be a fruitful seed;
Live truly, and thy life shall be
A great and noble creed.

— HORATIUS BONAR (1808-1890)[84]

Scottish author and writer of religious hymns

Being true to self and being true to God are absolutes for success. Nothing is worth compromising honor and truth.

To me the highest thing, after God, is my honor.

— LUDWIG VAN BEETHOVEN[85]

E. Know God:

The gods we worship write their names on our faces.[86]

Every human being was created with a void inside him, which can only be filled by knowing and acknowledging God and His creative power. Giving God reverence by allowing Him to guide the affairs of men and women is crucial to full success. When a person fully understands true philosophy and the intricate parts of the brain, he understands that there is a God whose power is unlimited. The wise person acknowledges Him and learns to follow His guidance.

A little philosophy inclineth man's mind to atheism; but depth in philosophy bringeth men's mind about to religion.
— FRANCIS BACON (1561-1626)
English professor, statesman, and jurist

Proverbs 4:7 declares: "Wisdom is the principal thing; therefore get wisdom: and with all thy getting get understanding." Get understanding; where does understanding originate? Proverbs 9:10 answers this question: "The fear of the LORD is the beginning of wisdom: and the knowledge of the holy is understanding." This is why it is so important to make daily Bible reading a part of your life!

History supplies us and is replete with the many successful leaders who acknowledged God and drew from His strength, as the following examples depict:

* The famous Henry Ford (1863-1947) made the statement: "I believe God is managing affairs and that He doesn't need any advice from me. With God in charge, I believe that everything will work out for the best in the end. So what is there to worry about?"[87]

* William James, the father of modern psychology, wrote to his friend, Professor Thomas Davidson, saying that as the years went by, he found himself "less and less able to get along without God."[88] One of his famous quotes is as follows: "We and God have business with each other; and in opening ourselves to His influence, our deepest destiny is fulfilled."

* Jack Dempsey, the famous heavyweight champion, said he never went to bed without praying, never ate a meal

without first thanking God for it, and always prayed every day when he was training for a bout. "Praying," he said, "helped me fight with courage and confidence."[89]

- When William IV of England died, a young girl was spending the night at the palace. They awakened her and told her that she was now the queen of England. As soon as she heard the news, she dropped to her knees and asked the heavenly Father to help and to guide her through all the years that were to follow. For sixty-four years, this girl, who was Queen Victoria, reigned over the British Empire. England never made greater progress than during her reign. A prince of India asked her what was the secret of England's power, and for her answer she quietly picked up a Book from the table nearby. "This is the secret," she said. The Book was God's Word, the Bible.
  — Told by GEORGE W. TRUETT[90]

- Robert Lewis of Fredricksburg, Virginia, was President George Washington's private secretary. During the first part of the presidency, he said that he accidentally witnessed Washington's private devotions, both morning and evening. He saw him in a kneeling position, with an open Bible before him; and he said that he believed such was his daily practice. His custom was to go to his library at four o'clock in the morning for devotions.[91]

I have felt His hand upon me in great trials and submitted to His guidance, and I trust that as He shall further open the way, I will be ready to walk therein, relying on His help and trusting in His goodness and wisdom.
  — ABRAHAM LINCOLN (1809-1865) [92]
  16th president of the United States (1861-65)

- *I have so fixed the habit of prayer in my mind that I never raise a glass of water to my lips without asking God's blessing, never seal a letter without putting a word of prayer under the seal, never take a letter from the post without a brief sending of my thoughts heavenward, never change my classes in the lecture-room without a minute's petition for the cadets who go out and for those who come in.*[93]
  — ANDREW STONEWALL JACKSON (1767-1845)
  7th President of the United States and famous American general

- *If the Word of Christ dwells in us it will make us helpers of others. It will so saturate and sweeten our thoughts, our dispositions, our tempers, and our feelings that the love of Christ will flow out in all our common speech. It will make our words gracious and kind.*[94]

  — REV. J. R. MILLER

- *It is impossible to rightly govern the world without God and the Bible.*[95]

  — GEORGE WASHINGTON (1732-1799)

  1st president of the United States (1789-97), known as the Father of His Country

- *Make it the first morning business of your life to understand some part of the Bible clearly, and make it your daily business to obey it in all that you do understand.*[96]

  — JOHN RUSKIN

When a person can acknowledge one's need of God and get in alignment with His high purposes, he or she will emerge a winner. There is strength in knowing God and his ways and in following the high road of true success.

The strength of a man consists in finding out the way in which God is going, and going in that way too.

— HENRY WARD BEECHER (1813-1887)

To know where one is going (direction), what one wants (purpose), his stuff (skill), himself, and God is knowledge. Knowledge is increased by reading, reason, experience, observation, listening, and keen alertness. It was said of Napoleon Bonaparte: "His passion for reading was carried to excess, and he eagerly devoured the contents of every book that fell his way."[97]

Reading is to the mind what exercise is to the body. As by the one, health is preserved, strengthened, and invigorated; by the other, virtue (which is the health of the mind) is kept alive, cherished and confirmed.

— ADDISON[98]

Anne Sullivan said of Helen Keller: "I am convinced that Helen's use of English is due largely to her familiarity with books. She often reads for two or three hours in succession, and then lays aside her book reluctantly. One day as we left the library I noticed that she appeared more serious than usual, and I asked the cause. 'I am thinking how much wiser we always are when we leave here than we are when we come,' was her reply.

"When asked why she loved books so much, she once replied: 'Because they tell me so much that is interesting about things I cannot see, and they are never tired or troubled like people. They tell me over and over what I want to know.' "[99]

SUCCESS STORY:

ABRAHAM LINCOLN

Abraham Lincoln is synonymous with learning and gaining knowledge. He made extraordinary efforts to attain knowledge while working on a farm, splitting rails for fences, and keeping store at New Salem, Illinois. Later his law partner said of him, "His ambition was a little engine that knew no rest." He had an insatiable appetite for knowledge.

Among the people of the settlement, bush farmers, and small tradesmen, he found a few books, which he borrowed eagerly. He read and reread, *Aesop's Fables*, learning to tell stories with a point and to argue by parables. He also read *Robinson Crusoe, The Pilgrim's Progress*, a short history of the United States, and Weem's *Life of Washington*. To the town constable's he went to read the Revised Statues of Indiana. Every printed page that fell into his hands he would greedily devour, and his family and friends watched him with wonder as the uncouth boy, after his daily work, crouched in a corner of the log cabin or outside under a tree, absorbed in a book. In this manner he began to gather some knowledge and sometimes would astonish his friends with remarks that startled them, leaving them in wonder as to where "Abe" could have gotten such queer notions.

He not only read everything he could find but also felt an impulse to write. He would sketch little essays with charcoal on a wooden shovel or on basswood shingles. Then he transferred them to paper, which was a scarce commodity in the Lincoln household. In his neighborhood he was gaining a reputation as a clever young man. He would often mount a stump in the field and keep the farmhands entertained with his speeches, which were sprinkled with excerpts from books he had read.

There is a good possibility that Lincoln would have never become President of the United States if he had not pursued his thirst for knowledge. It was partly the pursuit of knowledge that propelled him into his future.

SUCCESS NUGGETS:

Purposes, like eggs, unless they be hatched into action, will run into decay.
— SMILES[100]

There is nothing so costly as ignorance.
— HORACE MANN[101]

We should be as careful of the books we read, as of the company we keep. The dead very often have more power than the living.
— TYRON EDWARDS[102]

Think great thoughts. Cultivate the reading habit. The Bible is a wealth of literature. Read it daily. It will be an intellectual tonic. Store the galleries of your mind with pictures of great lives and deeds of the great. Have your own 'hall of fame.' Study over and over the influences which made for greatness in their lives. Come up under the shadow of their loftiness of thought, nobility of character and the sublimity of their courage.[103]

10
LEARN TO PRAY, FOR PRAYER IS POWER

"And all things, whatsoever ye shall ask in prayer, believing, ye shall receive" (Matthew 21:22).

Power in prayer is the greatest power in the world. It is greater than power of wealth, power of oratory, power of song, or any other power. You can see the greatest things happen through prayer. It is a privilege to pray. Prayer is a treasure house of good things. We are invited to come boldly to the throne room of God with our needs and petitions, and He will hear us.

Prayer gives strength when you feel you are fainting. Time spent in prayer brings joy when there is sorrow. Prayer is a release from pent-up tensions and problems. Prayer clears the vision, steadies the nerves, defines duty, and stiffens the purpose.

Prayer will inspire you to live each day as if it were your last, for when you pray you get a glimpse of eternity. Your world becomes larger. Prayer causes you to reach your goals. It helps to organize the mind. It energizes you! Prayer is like charging a battery. Prayer is energy.

Prayer will cause you to reach the highest level of achievement. It will help you be the master of a situation instead of having the situation master you. It will lift your thoughts to the level of winning.

Prayer is a place of refuge where one meets with God. It brings protection and safety to the one who prays. S. Chrysotom said it like this: "The man without prayer is as the fish out of water, and gasping for life." Just as the fish gasps for life without being in water, so do people fight for life's breath when they do not pray. They are gasping and struggling for life when they cut themselves off from spending time in the rivers of God's presence. Communion with God brings life and peace!

Without prayer, a person becomes a dry, thirsty land and opens himself up to depression. He is unprotected from spirits that would attach themselves to him. S. Chrysotom wrote the following: "The man without prayer is as a city without walls, and open to all attacks." Prayer is a spiritual covering for the mind and heart. In God's presence there are protection and healing.

Prayerlessness can cause frustration and a nagging sense of unhappiness because when people do not reach up and touch divinity through prayer, they chain themselves to a never-ending cycle of self. Prayer lets God come into your life and thoughts, and it brings new understanding of things.

Milton said, "The end of all learning is to know God, and out of that knowledge is to love and imitate Him." How can one know Him if they do not spend time with Him in prayer, and how can they become like Him if they do not know Him?

Prayer, if practiced by the masses, would totally change the world. There are miracles and answers to questions just waiting for them if they would only choose to pray to God and invite Him into their lives.

Prayer is the life line in God's blessed hands. How carefully he holds us in the darkest and most uncertain hours. But, oh, how safe we are. "He knoweth our frame. He remembereth that we are dust," "I will never leave thee nor forsake thee." "Fear thou not for I am with thee; be not dismayed. I am thy God. I will strengthen thee; yea, I will help thee; yea, I will uphold thee with the right hand of my righteousness." He was near Abraham on his mountain with Isaac. He was with Moses at the Red Sea. Everything came out just right with Jacob, Joseph and Benjamin. He was with Daniel in the den of lions; with the three Hebrew children. He refreshed Elijah by the coming of the angel. He never fails. He always has His own big, BIG plans. We can hold stead through prayer and how wonderfully everything will come out.[104]

More things are wrought by prayer
Than the world dreams of,
Wherefore let thy voice
Rise like a fountain for me night and day.
For what are men better than sheep or goats
That nourish a blind life within the brain,
If, knowing God, they lift not hands of prayer
Both for themselves and those who call them friend?
Bound by gold chains about the feet of God.
— ALFRED TENNYSON[105]

MEDICAL DOCTORS THOUGHTS ON PRAYER:

Many doctors attest to the power of prayer as the following paragraphs demonstrate:

Alexis Carrell, MD, a French surgeon and biologist who won the Nobel Prize for medical research in 1906, wrote an article in the March issue 1941 *Reader's Digest*. He entitled it "Prayer is Power." Following is a portion of that article:

Prayer is the most powerful form of energy that one can generate. The influence of prayer on the human mind and body is as demonstrable as that of secreting glands. Its results can be measured in terms of increased physical buoyancy, greater intellectual vigor, moral stamina, and a deep understanding of the realities underlying human relationships.

If you make a habit of sincere prayer, your life will be very noticeably and profoundly altered. Prayer stamps with its indelible mark our actions and demeanor. A tranquility of bearing, a facial and bodily repose, are observed in those who inner lives are thus enriched. Within the depths of consciousness a flame kindles. And man sees himself. He discovers his selfishness, his silly pride, his fears, his greed, his blunders. He develops a sense of moral obligation, intellectual humility. Thus begins a journey of the soul toward the realm of grace.

Prayer is a force as real as terrestrial gravity. As a physician, I have seen men, after all other therapy has failed, lifted out of disease and melancholy by the serene effort of prayer. It is the only power in the world that seems to overcome the so-called laws of nature; *the occasions on which prayer has dramatically done this have been termed* miracles. *Only in prayer do we achieve that complete and harmonious assembly of body, mind, and spirit which gives the frail human reed its unshakable strength.*[106]

George Schilling, MD, who practices internal medicine in Stockton, California, shared with me the following in an interview with him on March 4, 1996:

We have witnessed people who have been made better by prayer and strong belief. Prayer groups have prayed for some of my patients, and the prayer has helped them to be healed or their health improved. I have a couple who have been on the edge of death several times, and it was the prayers of people in prayer groups that have brought them back. I have another terminally ill lady whom I am treating who has cancer of the pancreas. She has strong belief in God and has a group praying for her and, to my amazement, is better. Their dramatic improvement cannot be explained scientifically.

Dr. Will Mayo of the world-famous Mayo Clinic said the following: "I have seen patients that were dead by all standards. We knew they could not live. But I have seen a minister come to the bedside and do something for him that I could not do, although I have done everything in my professional power. But something touched some immortal spark in him and in defiance of medical knowledge and materialistic common sense, that patient *lived!*"[107]

Larry Dossey, MD, wrote about something that happened during his residency at Parkland Memorial Hospital in Dallas, Texas. He encountered his first patient with terminal cancer. The cancer had spread throughout both of the man's lungs. Dr. Dossey told him what treatments were available but what little they could do. The man chose no treatment. Yet, whenever Dr. Dossey stopped by his hospital bedside, the man was surrounded by visitors from his church, who were singing and praying.

A year later, when Dr. Dossey was working somewhere else, a colleague at Parkland called to ask if he wanted to see his old patient. Dr. Dossey wrote back, "See him? I couldn't believe he was still alive. At the hospital I studied his chest X rays. I was stunned. The man's lungs were completely clear. There was no sign of cancer."

"His therapy has been remarkable," said the radiologist, looking over my shoulder. *Therapy?* I thought. *There wasn't any unless you consider prayer.*

Dr. Dossey wrote, "I had long given up the faith of my childhood. Now I believed in the power of modern medicine. Prayer seemed an arbitrary frill. So I put the incident out of my mind. Years passed and I became chief of staff at a large urban hospital. Then one day in the late 1980s I came across a study done by Randolph Byrd, a cardiologist at San Francisco General Hospital. To my amazement I found an enormous body of evidence: more than one hundred experiments exhibiting the criteria of good science. . . . Scientists, including physicians, can have blind spots. The power of prayer seemed to be one of them."[108]

FAMOUS PEOPLE'S THOUGHTS ON PRAYER

I believe it is impossible to live well without prayer, and that prayer is the necessary condition of a good, peaceful, and happy life. The Gospels indicate how one should pray, and what prayer should consist of.
— LEO TOLSTOY[109]

In the midst of President Woodrow Wilson's difficulties in international negotiations, he, too, felt the need of divine guidance. When Mr. Wilson arrived at a cabinet meeting, his face wore a solemn look. It was evident that serious affairs of the nation were on his mind. He said to the cabinet members: "I don't know whether you men believe in prayer or not. I do. Let us pray and ask the help of God." The twenty-eighth President of the United States fell upon his knees with the members of the cabinet, and offered a prayer to God for help.
— TOLD BY AQUILLA WEBB[110]

I have been driven many times to my knees by the overwhelming conviction that I had nowhere else to go. My own wisdom and that of all about me seemed insufficient for the day.
— ABRAHAM LINCOLN [111]
(During the Civil War)

In 1787 when the Constitutional Convention was on the verge of total failure over the issue of whether small states should have the same representation as large states, Benjamin Franklin offered a suggestion. He said, "Gentlemen, I have lived a long time and am convinced that God governs in the affairs of men. If a sparrow cannot fall to the ground without His notice, is it probable that an empire can rise without His aid? I move that prayer imploring the assistance of heaven be held every morning before we proceed to business."[112]

The motion carried. From then on prayer was offered each morning. The change after prayer was introduced was so dramatic that in a short while a compromise was reached which is still in effect today.

I can take my telescope and look millions and millions of miles into space, but I can lay it aside and go into my room, shut the door, get down on my knees in earnest prayer, and see more of heaven and get closer to God than I can assisted by all the telescopes and material agencies on earth.
—SIR ISAAC NEWTON[113]

In conversation with Professor S. F. B. Morse, the inventor of the telegraph, the Rev. George W. Hervey asked this question: "Professor Morse, when you were making your experiments yonder in your room in the university, did you ever come to a stand, not knowing what to do next?"

"Oh, yes, more than once," he answered.

"And at such times, what did you do next?" asked Rev. Hervey.

"I may answer you in confidence, sir," said the professor, "but it is a matter of which the public knows nothing. I prayed for more light."

"And the light generally came?"

"Yes, and may I tell you that when flattering honors come to me from America and Europe on account of the invention which bears my name, I never felt I deserved them. I had made a valuable application of electricity, not because I was superior to other men, but solely because God, who meant it for mankind, must reveal it to someone, and was pleased to reveal it to me."

In view of these facts, it is not surprising that the inventor's first telegraph message, sent over a forty-mile line between Washington and Baltimore, was "What hath God wrought?"[114]

TRUE STORIES OF ANSWERED PRAYER
One Sunday night in April 1912, an American woman was very weary yet could not sleep because of an oppression of fear. At

last she felt a burden of prayer and with tremendous earnestness began to pray for her husband then in the mid-Atlantic, homeward bound on the *Titanic*. As the hours went by, she could get no assurance and kept on praying in an agony until about 5:00 in the morning when a great peace possessed her and she slept.

Meanwhile her husband, Colonel Gracie, was among the doomed hundreds who were trying frantically to launch the lifeboats from the great ship, whose vitals had been torn out by an iceberg. He had given up all hope of being saved himself and was doing his best to help the women and children. He wished that he could get a last message through to his wife and cried from his heart, "Good-bye, my darling." Then as the ship plunged to her watery grave, he was sucked down in the giant whirlpool. Instinctively he began to swim under water, ice cold as it was.

Suddenly he came to the surface and found himself near an overturned lifeboat. Along with several others, he climbed aboard and was picked up by another lifeboat, about 5:00 in the morning, the very time that peace came to his praying wife![115]

The two most famous legions in the Roman army were the Tenth Legion and the Thundering Legion. The Tenth Legion was composed of Caesar's veteran shock troops. In every great emergency, it was upon that legion he called, and it never failed him. The Thundering Legion was the name given to the Militine Legion in the days of the philosopher emperor—yet one of the worst persecutors of the church—Marcus Aurelius.

Tertullian tells how the legion won that name, the "Thundering Legion." In AD 176, the army of the emperor was engaged in a campaign against the Germans. In their march the Romans found themselves encircled by precipitous mountains, which were occupied by their savage enemies. In addition to this danger, the army was tormented by thirst because of the drought. Then the commander of the Praetorian Guard informed the emperor that the Militine Legion was made up of Christians and that they believed in the power of prayer.

"Let them pray, then," said the emperor. The soldiers of the legion bowed on the ground and earnestly besought God in the name of Christ to deliver the Roman army. They had scarcely risen from their knees when a great thunderstorm arose, accompanied by hail. The storm drove the barbarians out of their strongholds, and, descending from the mountains, they

117

entreated the Romans for mercy. His army delivered from death at the hands of the barbarians, all delivered from death by the drought, the emperor decreed that this legion should be thereafter called the "Thundering Legion." He also abated somewhat his persecution of the Christians.[116]

— Told By C.E. Macartney

Millions of copies of Warner Sallman's *Head of Christ* painting hang in homes around the world. The picture presents Jesus as a man of strong personality, rugged health, with the marks of character and leadership. Following is the artist's life that shaped his view of Jesus:

In 1917, the young artist was told by his physician, "You have tuberculosis of the lymph glands. Without surgery I believe you have about three months to live!"

Warner Sallman left the office in a daze. He was concerned for the young singer who had recently become his bride and for their baby that was soon to be born. When he told his wife about the doctor's prognosis, she said, "We will pray and thank God for the three months. We will ask Him to use us to the limit, and if He will mercifully give us more time, we shall be grateful for it." Together they knelt in trusting prayer.

A marvelous healing took place. Warner Sallman never needed surgery. For many years he remained in robust health, dedicating his life to Christ.[117]

A miracle took place for Lloyd B. Wilhide of Keymar, Maryland. It was just an ordinary day, when crisis overtook him and he prayed to God for help. His words are as follows:

"Ask and it shall be given you," Jesus said. I've always believed this but never so totally as the day of the accident in 1978. I was seventy-five years old. The grass on our 121-acre dairy farm needed cutting, so I hitched a set of mower blades to my tractor and went to work. The tractor was huge, and for added traction on our up and down Maryland terrain, its rear wheels were filled with five hundred pounds of fluid, and a two-hundred-pound weight hung from each hub.

When I finished the job, I was on a slight uphill grade near our chicken house. I switched off the ignition and climbed down from the high seat. I was unfastening the mower blades when the tractor started moving backward.

118

I tried to twist around and jump up on the seat, but I didn't make it. The tractor's drawbar hit me in the knees, knocking me flat, and the seven-hundred-pound left wheel rolled over my chest and stopped on top of it. I struggled for breath. The pain was agonizing. I knew I was facing death, and I made my request.

"Please, God," I begged, "release me."

At that moment the tractor began to move. It went forward enough to free my chest, and to my astonishment it moved *uphill!*

My dog and then a farmhand found me, and after six broken ribs, two fractures, and twelve days in the hospital, I was back home, talking with the Maryland state trooper who called to investigate the accident. "I won't try to explain it officially," he told me, "why a dozen men couldn't have moved that tractor off you."

Twelve men or twelve hundred, it didn't matter. Asking God's help did.[118]

Prayer pulls the rope below and the great bell rings above in the ears of God. Some scarcely stir the bell, for they pray so languidly; others give an occasional pluck at the rope; but he who wins with heaven is the man who grabs the rope boldly, and pulls continuously, with all his might.
—SPURGEON[119]

SUCCESS STORY:

JAMES LEWIS KRAFT

James Lewis Kraft was born in Ontario, Canada, in 1874 to Mennonite parents. He learned to pray at an early age and was always God-conscious. At the age of twenty-eight, he moved to Chicago. He was stranded with only sixty-five dollars in his pocket, so with that he bought a horse and wagon. He then went to the wholesale warehouse district and bought cheese, which he took into the city and sold to small stores, saving merchants from having to make the trip.

He began working on a special cheese that became known as processed cheese and was granted a patent for this in 1916. Walter B. Knight wrote the following about Kraft: "Years ago a young man began a small cheese business in Chicago. He failed. He was deeply in debt. 'You didn't take God into your business. You have not worked with Him,' said a Christian friend to him. Then Mr. Kraft thought, 'If God wants to run the cheese business, He can do it, and I'll work for Him and with Him!' From that moment, God became the senior partner in his business. The business grew and prospered and became the largest cheese concern in the world!"[120]

James L. Kraft, Canadian/American entrepreneur and inventor, helped to create Kraft Foods Inc. He served as the company's president from 1909 until his death in 1953. The Kraft blog on the Internet has this to say about Kraft Foods: "Hard work, imagination and a commitment to bring the world its favorite foods have helped us grow into a company that touches more than a billion people in more than 150 countries."

This is certainly success! When you take a God-fearing young man with only sixty-five dollars, who made God his senior partner, and see his dream become a business that today touches more than a billion people; that is success!

SUCCESS NUGGETS:

PRAY WITHOUT CEASING

Unanswered yet? But you are not unheeded:
The promises of God forever stand;
To Him our days and years alike are equal;
Have faith in God! It is your Lord's command.
Hold on to Jacob's angel, and your prayer
Shall bring a blessing down sometime, somewhere.

Unanswered yet? Faith cannot be unanswered;
Her feet are firmly planted on the Rock;
Amid the wildest storms she stands undaunted,
Nor quails before the loudest thunder shock.
She knows Omnipotence has heard her prayer,
And cries, "It shall be done sometime, somewhere."
— OPHELIA GUYON BROWNING[123]

I exhort therefore, first of all, that supplications, prayers, intercessions, thanksgiving, be made for all men.
— I TIMOTHY 2:1 (AMERICAN STANDARD VERSION)

I refuse to live a cheap life and think chaffy thoughts. I refuse to surrender to worry, fear, prejudice and bitterness. I resolve to bathe my mind with the waters of peace and love. God is my guide, my shield and my exceeding great reward. I refuse to permit anything small, mean, coarse or vulgar to remain in my heart or mind. My soul shall breathe only the breath of God.

— DEAN C. DUTTON[121]

Prayer gives you courage to make the decisions you must make in crisis and then the confidence to leave the result to a Higher Power.

— GENERAL EISENHOWER[122]

11

BE ON FIRE

WITH AN IDEA

"Nothing will be restrained from them, which they have imagined to do" (Genesis 11:6).

In time, the generation after the Flood became a very godless people, and they were intent in building a tower into the heavens. God recognized the power of thought and said nothing could keep them from doing what they were on fire in the minds to do. That is, nothing except God. God had to confuse them because they were not building on God's principles, and their ideas were not in alignment with God's.

Ideas are fascinating. They are the engineers of thoughts, which cause magical changes in something that could be considered useless. Ideas are translated into substance, such as when a bare piece of land is changed into a beautifully landscaped garden, or a useless piece of metal becomes the shell of an airplane.

If a person who has an idea about something, and he or she is on fire with it, the end results are limitless as to what can transpire. The passion behind the idea brings fulfillment to it.

Be on Fire with an Idea

A pile of rocks ceases to be a rock pile when somebody contemplates it with the idea of a cathedral in mind.
— ANTOINE DE SAINT-EXUPERY (1900-1944)
French writer and aviator

Ideas should not be cast aside like pieces of driftwood but should be thought upon carefully, for ideas are like a light that shines into a person's brain, bringing enlightenment that opens a door for great things. A person never knows what idea will be the one that becomes the driving force for a passionate pursuit of purpose.

Bring ideas in and entertain them royally, for one of them may be the king.
— MARK VAN DOREN (1894-1972)
American writer and editor

Ideas that sometimes flash into the brain, if not entertained, are forgotten and never come back quite the same way. They bring a flash of excitement about a certain thing that causes one to move out of boredom into eager anticipation. Ideas cannot be regulated to a time clock but must be taken as soon as they come. They are not stored as on a tape recorder, where they can be recorded and at a later date be replayed. Grab them when they come and write them down, for they are as gold to the human soul.

Seize the moment of excited curiosity on any subject to solve your doubts; for if you let it pass, the desire may never return.
— WILLIAM WIRT (1772-1834)
American lawyer

If the fire of an idea is not fanned, it is possible for it to go out instead of igniting into noble purpose. An idea must not only be lit, it must be kept burning as well. Aflame, ideas can change a world. The blazing passion is what causes the purpose to materialize.

A good idea is like a match. It is useless unless you strike it into flame.
— AUTHOR UNKNOWN

The discoveries of Russian Elie Metchnikoff concerning the digestion of bacteria by white corpuscles, the so-called phagocytosis, were sparked by an idea, which he struck into a flame. Born near Kharkov in 1845, he was trained as a zoologist and acquired most of his knowledge on his travels to Italy, North Africa, and France. Interested in physiological phenomena akin to digestion, he had observed the manner in which amoebas absorb particles. This is what eventually inspired him to see an analogy between this absorption he had observed and the function of the white corpuscles. He wrote in his recollections:

One day when the whole family had gone to the circus, I was observing the life of the mobile cells of a transparent starfish larva, when I was suddenly illuminated by a new thought. I had the idea that analogous cells probably served to defend the organism against harmful intruders. Sensing that there was something very interesting in this, I became so excited that I began to walk very fast, even going to the seashore to collect my thoughts. I said to myself that a thorn placed into the body of a starfish larva, which has neither blood vessels nor a nervous system, should be very quickly surrounded by mobile cells, as can be observed in humans when they have a splinter in a finger. No sooner said than done. In the little garden at our house I took several thorns from a rose bush and immediately placed them under the skin of several superb starfish larvae that were as transparent as water. I was so excited that I did not sleep at all that night, waiting for the results of my experiment. The next morning I was overjoyed to find that it had fully succeeded.[124]

Another example of a person who had an idea burn within the brain was Harriet Beecher Stowe.

I will write something. I will if I live.
— HARRIET BEECHER STOWE (1811-1896)
American author

And write she did! Harriet Beecher was born in Litchfield, Connecticut, the seventh child of the nine children of the famous Congregational minister Lyman Beecher. The crusading Beechers were one of the best-known families of the American nineteenth century.

Harriet was educated at the Hartford Female Seminary, kept by her elder sister Catherine. She entered the academy at the age of eleven, and four years later she became an assistant teacher. She continued to teach in Cincinnati, where the family moved in 1832. There she met and married Calvin Ellis Stowe, a professor of biblical literature, and gave birth to seven children.

Her first book, entitled *Primary Geography for Children*, was published in 1833. Soon she was publishing domestic stories and

Be on Fire with an Idea

sketches of life in New England. In 1850, the Stowe family moved to Brunswick, Maine. That same year, the United States Congress passed the Fugitive Slave Act, requiring all citizens to aid in the capture of runaway slaves. No one was more outraged than author Harriet Beecher Stowe, who was determined to write something about this, "miserable wicked fugitive slave business."

She began *Uncle Tom's Cabin; or, Life among the Lowly*. Serialized in an antislavery weekly from June 1851 to April 1852, *Uncle Tom's Cabin* was published in March 1952. It became the biggest bestseller of the nineteenth century.

It was Dronais, a pupil of Jacques Louis David (1748-1825), the leading French painter during the French Revolution and the Napoleonic era, who had the same passion that characterized Elie and Harriet. He was often at his studies from four in the morning until night. "Painting or nothing!" was the cry of this enthusiast. "First fame, then amusement," was another one of his sayings.

Each person has a thought center where ideas come as a flash. The center is like a small kingdom that rules the whole body. The brain controls the bodily functions, and the thought center entertains emotions, ideas, feelings, and moods. This center in some people is very drowsy, unawake to any great passion. They live in a kingdom that is asleep.

Every human mind is a great slumbering power until awakened by a keen desire and by definite resolution to do.
— EDGAR F. ROBERTS

There is an energy that is generated when ideas are masterfully pursued or brought into daily focus. Ideas work as a venture that excites the human mind and causes one to live in a state of enthusiasm that energizes. This comes from purpose that has been fired by an idea.

The hot place in a man's [or woman's] consciousness, the group of ideas to which he [or she] devotes himself [or herself] and from which he [or she] works, call it the habitual center of his [or her] personal energy.
— WILLIAM JAMES (1842-1910)[125]

When a thought or idea is born, there is the venturing forth into uncharted seas of adventure, for once an idea blazes in the

126

brain, there can never be the same lackadaisical approach to life. It enriches, enlarges, and stretches the human mind. The quest becomes greater than any sacrifice, pain, or obstacles.

Man's mind stretched to a new idea never goes back to its original dimensions.
— OLIVER WENDELL HOLMES, SR. (1909-1894)
American poet and writer

If everyone had the same philosophy as Robert Frost, the social and academic climate of many towns and regions would be changed.

Some men see things as they are and say why?
I dream of things that never were and say why not?
— ROBERT FROST (1874-1963)
Popular American poet

Major Alexander P. de Seversky, a famous aviation expert and author of *Victory through Air Power,* lost a leg in World War I. As a result of this, he wrote the following:

I discovered early that the hardest thing to overcome is not a physical disability but the mental condition which it induces. The world, I found, has a way of taking a man pretty much at his own rating. If he permits his loss to make him embarrassed and apologetic, he will draw embarrassment from others. But if he gains his own respect, the respect of those around him comes easily.[126]

Alexander de Seversky, pilot, inventor, designer, businessman, and visionary author, led one of the most varied lives of his times. On June 7, 1894, he was born a Russian nobleman. At age fourteen, he entered the Imperial Russian Naval Academy and already knew how to fly, as his father had been one of the first Russians to own a plane. He graduated in 1914 with an engineering degree and was serving at sea as a lieutenant in the Imperial Navy of Russia when World War I began. He attacked a German destroyer in the Gulf of Riga but was shot down before he could drop his bombs. When his plane crashed, the bombs exploded, badly wounding him. He lost one leg below the knee. Equipped with a wooden leg, he was deemed unfit for combat duty. He made a spectacular unauthorized flight at an air show to demonstrate that he could still fly but was arrested for his efforts. In 1916 Seversky returned to combat duty because of the czar's personal intervention.

127

In February 1917, he assumed command of the 2nd Naval Fighter Detachment until an accident with a horse-drawn wagon broke his good leg. In all, he flew fifty-seven sorties and shot down six German aircraft (some say thirteen) to become Russia's top naval ace.

In March 1918, Seversky arrived in the United States to serve as assistant naval attaché at the Russian embassy. He then chose to make America his home and went to work for the War Department as an aeronautical engineer and test pilot. He filed 364 patent claims, among them the first gyroscopically stabilized bombsight, which he developed with Sperry Gyroscope Company in 1923. In 1927 he became a United States citizen and gained a major's commission in the US Army Air Corps Reserve.

He was largely responsible for the creation of the P-35, the first modern fighter, which was introduced in 1935. He formed the Seversky Aircraft Corporation but later was forced out of this because of financial loss. He then began to write and give speeches on airpower. After World War II, he was awarded the Medal of Merit by President Harry Truman. In 1952, he formed Seversky Electroaton Corporation, a company focused on protecting the United States from nuclear attack. When he died on August 24, 1974, he was well respected for his contribution to America's airpower.

Seversky was on fire with an idea, and it entered into all that he did or attempted to do. He was called on to be speaker at many banquets because of his homespun style of speaking, but no matter what the subject, he always got around to mentioning something about airpower. The fire of his ideas could not be extinguished either by time or by circumstances. If he were alive today, he would be known as a thinker outside of the box.

THE THINKER

Back of the beating hammer
By which the steel is wrought,
Back of the workshop's clamor
The seeker may find the Thought—
The Thought that is ever master
Of iron and steam and steel,
That rises above disaster
And tramples it under heel!

The drudge may fret and tinker
Or labor with lusty blows,
But back of him stands the Thinker,
The clear-eyed man who knows;
For into each plow or saber,
Each piece and part and whole,
Must go the Brains of Labor,
Which gives the work a soul!

Back of the motors humming,
Back of the bells that sing,
Back of the hammers drumming,
Back of the cranes that swing,
There is the eye which scans them
Watching through stress and strain,
There is the Mind which plans them—
Back of the brawn, the Brain!

Might of the roaring boiler,
Force of the engine's thrust,
Strength of the sweating toiler—
Greatly in these we trust.
But back of them stands the Schemer,
The Thinker who drives things through;
Back of the job—the Dreamer
Who's making the dream come true!
— BERTON BRALEY (1882-1966)[127]
American poet

SUCCESS STORY:

DALE CARNEGIE

Lowell Thomas wrote the following in 1958 about a man with an idea that changed his life:

Dale Carnegie's own career, filled with sharp contrasts, is a striking example of what a man can accomplish when he is obsessed with an original idea and afire with enthusiasm.

Born on a Missouri farm ten miles from a railway, he never saw a streetcar until he was twelve years old; yet, at forty-six, he was familiar with the far-flung corners of the earth. This Missouri lad who once picked strawberries and cut cockleburs for five cents an hour is now paid a dollar a minute for training the executives of large corporations in the art of self-expression.

This erstwhile cowboy who once punched cattle and branded calves and rode fences out in western South Dakota later went to London and put on shows under the patronage of His Royal Highness, the Prince of Wales.

This chap who was a total failure the first half-dozen times that he tried to speak in public later became my personal manager. Much of my success has been due to training under Dale Carnegie.

Young Carnegie had to struggle for an education, for hard luck was always battering away at the old farm in northwest Missouri. Year after year, the "102" River rose and drowned the corn and swept away the hay. Season after season, the fat hogs sickened and died from cholera, the bottom fell out of the market for cattle and mules, and the bank threatened to foreclose the mortgage.

Sick with discouragement, the family sold out and bought another farm near the State Teachers' College at Warrensburg, Missouri. Board and room could be had in town for a dollar a day, but young Carnegie couldn't afford it. So he stayed on the farm and commuted on horseback three miles to college each day. At home, he milked the cows, cut the wood, fed the hogs, and studied his Latin verbs by the light of a coal-oil lamp until his eyes blurred and he began to nod.

Even when he got to bed at midnight, he set the alarm for three o'clock. His father bred pedigreed Duroc-Jersey hogs — and there was danger, during the bitter cold nights, of the young pigs' freezing to death; so they were put in a basket, covered with a gunny sack, and set behind the kitchen stove. True to their nature, the pigs demanded a hot meal at three AM. So when the alarm went off, Dale Carnegie crawled out of the blankets, took the basket of pigs out to their mother, waited for them to nurse, and then brought them back to the warmth of the kitchen stove.

There were six hundred students in State Teachers' College, and Dale Carnegie was one of the isolated half-dozen who couldn't afford to board in town. He was ashamed of the poverty that made it necessary for him to ride back to the farm and milk the cows every night. He was ashamed of his coat, which was too tight, and his trousers, which were too short. Rapidly developing an inferiority complex, he looked about for certain groups in college that enjoyed influence and prestige—the football and baseball players and the chaps who won the debating and public-speaking contests.

Realizing that he had no flair for athletics, he decided to win one of the speaking contests. He spent months preparing his talks. He practiced as he sat in the saddle galloping to college and back; he practiced his speeches as he milked the cows; and then he mounted a bale of hay in the barn and with great gusto and gestures harangued the frightened pigeons. . . .

But in spite of all his earnestness and preparation, he met with defeat after defeat. He was eighteen at the time—sensitive and proud. He became so discouraged, so depressed that he even thought of suicide. And then suddenly he began to win, not one contest but every speaking contest in college.

Other students pleaded with him to train them; and they won also.

Graduating from college, he started selling correspondence courses to the ranchers among the sand hills of Western Nebraska and eastern Wyoming.

In spite of all his boundless energy and enthusiasm, he couldn't make the grade. He became so discouraged that he went to his hotel room in Alliance, Nebraska, in the middle of the day, threw himself across the bed, and wept with despair. He longed to go back to college, he longed to retreat from the harsh battle of life; but he couldn't. So he resolved to go to Omaha and get another job. He didn't have the money for a railroad ticket so he traveled on a freight train, feeding and watering two carloads of wild horses in return for his passage. Landing in South Omaha, he got a job selling bacon and soap and lard for Armour and Company. His territory was up among the Badlands and the cow and Indian country of western South Dakota. He covered his territory by freight train and on stage coach and on horseback and slept in pioneer hotels where the only partition between the rooms was a sheet of muslin. . . .

Within two years, he had taken an unproductive territory that stood in the twenty-fifth place and boosted it to first place among all the twenty-nine car routes leading out of South Omaha. Armour and Company offered to promote him, saying: "You have achieved what seemed impossible." But he refused the promotion and resigned—resigned, went to New York, studied at the American Academy of Dramatic Arts, and toured the country playing the role of Dr. Hartley in *Polly of the Circus.*

He would never be a Booth or a Barrymore. He had the good sense to recognize that. So back he went to sales work again, dispensing automobile trucks for the Packard Motor Car Company.

He knew nothing about machinery and cared nothing about it. Dreadfully unhappy, he had to scourge himself to his task each day. He longed to have time to study, to write the books he had dreamed about writing back in college. So he resigned. He was going to spend his days writing stories and novels and support himself by teaching in a night school.

Teaching what? As he looked back and evaluated his college work, he saw that his training in public speaking had done more to give him confidence, courage, poise, and the ability to meet and deal with people in business than had all the rest of his college courses put together. So he urged the YMCA schools in New York to give him a chance to conduct courses in public speaking for businessmen.

What? Make orators out of businessmen? Absurd. They knew. They had tried such courses—and they had always failed.

When they refused to pay him a salary of two dollars a night, he agreed to teach on a commission basis and take a percentage of the net profits. And inside of three years they were paying him thirty dollars a night on that basis—instead of two.

The course grew. The other YMC organizations heard of it, then other cities. Dale Carnegie soon became a glorified circuit rider, covering New York, Philadelphia, Baltimore, and later London and Paris. All the textbooks were too academic and impractical for the businessmen who flocked to his courses. Nothing daunted, he sat down and wrote one, entitled *Public Speaking and Influencing Men in Business.*[128]

On October 22, 1912, he started his first class. In 1933, Leon Shimkin, general manager of Simon and Schuster, Inc., enrolled in the course in Larchmont, New York. He was impressed not only with the speaking aspects of the training but also with the benefits of the human-relations principles. He saw great possibilities for a book. He suggested to Dale Carnegie that he gather all the material he had been teaching his students and adapt it for a book.

On November 12, 1936, *How to Win Friends and Influence People* was published, and it became an overnight success. Dale Carnegie became a name known in every household. The book sold over a million copies in less than a year and was printed in fourteen languages. For ten years it stayed on *The New York Times'* bestseller list, an all-time record for any book.

His ideas did not fit the normal way of doing things, but they were ablaze with new concepts that would make him, even to this day, a much sought-after author.

SUCCESS NUGGETS:

There are no great and small. We fancy others greater than ourselves because they light the divine spark given them, and we do not. It is because we minimize ourselves that we do not accomplish. We do not realize the power of the positions in which we are placed.
— RALPH WALDO EMERSON[129]

Except a living man there is nothing more wonderful than a book! a message to us from the dead — from human souls we never saw, who lived, perhaps, thousands of miles away. And yet these, in those little sheets of paper, speak to us, arouse us, terrify us, teach us, comfort us, open their hearts to us as brothers.
— CHARLES KINGSLEY[130]

True courage is the result of reasoning. A brave mind is always impregnable. Resolution lies more in the head than in the veins; and a just sense of honor and of infamy, of duty and of religion, will carry us farther than all the force of mechanism.
— JEREMY COLLIER[131]

12
LEARN TO OVERCOME OBSTACLES

"This is the victory that overcometh the world, even our faith" (I John 5:4).

Obstacles have been and always will be part of the structure of life. An obstacle can be defined as a barrier, blockage, difficulty, or hindrance. It is something in the way of progress: a hurdle to be jumped over or cleared. Instead of a stumbling block, an obstacle can become a stepping-stone to greater things, as noted by the following great educator:

> *No matter how poor you are, how black you are, or how obscure your present position, each one should remember there is a chance for him, and the more difficulties he has to overcome, the greater can be his success.*
> — BOOKER T. WASHINGTON

A goal is the guiding force of life. When one is knocked down by opposition or overwhelmed by barriers and difficulties, a vision problem ensues. The eyes that looked ahead and focused on a goal have now shifted to the obstacle; they lose sight of the greater purpose and, if one is not careful, drown in the lesser condition. The objectives or aspirations have not changed. They are still out there, doing their best to beckon to those who lose heart. During this time it is important to remember that the goal must be greater than the obstacle.

> *Obstacles are those frightful things you see when you take your eyes off your goal.*
>
> —HENRY FORD (1863-1947)
>
> Developer of the mass-produced "Model T" automobile
> He pioneered the use of assembly-line methods.

When one resolves that nothing can stop him from reaching his goal, somehow the barriers, one by one, are dissolved before the resolute force of an individual's will. If in the storm of life one can hang on to the reason for the storm, all will be well. Purposes, goals, and aspirations will definitely bring hindrances and difficulties. That is all part of life, but they should not be allowed to put out the fire of an idea. Let them be used only as fuel to succeed.

> *Obstacles cannot crush me; every obstacle yields to stern resolve.*

Obstacles can defeat a lesser person, or it can make one stronger. If there were never any pressures or difficulties, there would never be growth. The challenging things cause people to develop and to expand. The mind is stretched during difficulty; whereas, a mind that never encounters a storm becomes soft and restricted.

> *You never will be the person you can be if pressure, tension, and discipline are taken out of your life.*
>
> —JAMES G. BILKEY

It does not matter the obstacle; what matters is the resolve of the one facing the obstacle. Difficulties should be earmarked as challenges or something to be conquered and overcome. Life's circumstances can make one feel trampled upon, but the strong just keep fighting back until they win.

> *Some minds seem almost to create themselves, springing up under every disadvantage and working their solitary but irresistible way through a thousand obstacles.*
>
> —WASHINGTON IRVING (1783-1859)
>
> American author and diplomat

Irving was the first American writer to gain fame in other nations, as well as at home. He went to England in 1815 to run the Liverpool branch of the family hardware business but could not save it when the whole firm failed. Thereupon, with the encouragement of Walter Scott, Irving turned definitely to literature. His stories and essays reflect his genuine charm, sense of humor, and pleasant disposition. His more famous works were *Rip van Winkle, Ichabod Crane,* and *Oliver Goldsmith.* He was the last of eleven children. He loved poetry and books of travel but disliked school and left it when he was sixteen.

He returned to New York in 1933 and wrote about the American West. Irving established himself at his estate, Sunnyside, near Tarrytown, New York, until he was sent to Madrid as American minister to Spain (1842-1846). Once more at Sunnyside, he wrote a biography of Goldsmith (1849) and labored at his biography of George Washington (five volumes) (1855-1859), which he completed just before his death.

Irving's failure at keeping the family-owned business afloat was a turning point in his career. He refused to let life stomp on him and quickly turned to the calling of his life: writing, and at that he succeeded.

It is not the discouragement or the temporary setbacks that are most important; more importantly is the successful overcoming of the things that bring discouragement. Some people have more to overcome than others. It is a strange fact that sometimes those who have more ability are inclined to lean on that ability and not reach their potential; whereas on the other hand, those with less ability, work harder until they surpass those who had it easy. They are the true winners: those who have overcome much and succeeded.

I have learned that success is to be measured not so much by the position that one has reached in life as by the obstacles which he has overcome while trying to succeed.
— BOOKER T. WASHINGTON[132]

One who overcame much was Helen Keller. Anne Sullivan shares the following incident from the life of Helen, which demonstrates her ability to overcome obstacles that were in the way of her success.

Not long ago I tried to show her how to build a tower with her blocks. As the design was somewhat complicated, the slightest jar made the structure fall. After a time I became discouraged, and told her I was afraid she could not make it stand, but that I would build it for her;

but she did not approve of this plan. She was determined to build the tower herself; and for nearly three hours she worked away, patiently gathering up the blocks whenever they fell, and beginning over again, until at last her perseverance was crowned with success. The tower stood complete in every part.[133]

Oftentimes the very things that cause people to stop and think, the troubles that will not go away, or the adverse situations are the factors that bring out the best in them. It is the thing that causes one to reach into the inner consciousness and draw out something that was hidden by more comfortable times.

Adversity is the midwife of genius.
—NAPOLEON (1769-1821)
Emperor of France (1804-15)

Everyone chooses how he or she reacts to adversity. The negative options are to rebel or to feel sorry for self. To rebel against something that is unchangeable is a fight that is never won. It is the duty of the individual to see what can be changed and to work at changing it. Adversity should be a challenge to overcome all odds and to gain victory over defeat. There is nothing that can stand in the way of someone with a will to overcome, except of course, God! To achieve "in spite of" is heralded as a great success.

Rebellion against your handicaps gets you nowhere. Self-pity gets you nowhere. One must have the adventurous daring to accept oneself as a bundle of possibilities and undertake the most interesting game in the world — making the most of one's best.
—HARRY EMERSON FOSDICK (1878-1969)[134]
Clergyman and author

It would take many books to contain all the stories of those who have prevailed and attained even when it seemed an impossibility to do so. Several are listed below who belong in those books:

- *Alexander Pope* (1688-1744) was a hopeless invalid, unable to stand without the aid of a cruel brace, but became a famous English poet. He was deformed at age twelve.

- *Theodore Roosevelt* (1858-1919) was a sickly, puny child with scarcely a chance for maturity. He was afflicted with asthma and many times lay choking in his father's arms. He lived to become the twenty-sixth President of the United States of America (1901-1909).

- *Stephen A. Douglas* (1813-1861) was a hunchback who became a famous American statesman.

- *Thomas Edison* (1847-1931) lost most of his hearing at about eight years of age and, though struggling with deafness his whole life, perfected the phonograph.

- *John Milton* (1608-1674), blind, wrote England's greatest poem. In 1667, he published his masterpiece, *Paradise Lost*. After he became totally blind, he composed his *Treatise on Christian Doctrine*, and a still more extraordinary enterprise was that of the Latin dictionary, along with *Paradise Lost*.

- *Franklin D. Roosevelt* (1882-1945), even though crippled by infantile paralysis, became the thirty-second President of the United States (1933-1945).

- *Ben Jonson* (1573-1637) was a boy so ugly and ridiculously clothed that he was tormented by his schoolmates. He spent his time reading to forget his misery. At eighteen he worked as a bricklayer. But he finally won the acclaim and esteem of England. He was honored by Queen Elizabeth, was decorated by King James, and was one of the most brilliant playwrights and poets England ever produced.

- *Oliver Goldsmith* (1731-1774) was regarded as a stupid blockhead in the village school. When he finally got a degree from college, he was the lowest on the list. He was rejected for the ministry. He tried law with the same result. He borrowed a suit of clothes to take an examination as a hospital mate, failed, and pawned his clothes. He lived in garrets, failing at everything he tried. Only one thing he wanted to do—write. This he did and rose above the handicaps of illness, poverty, and obscurity to high rank among the greatest writers of all time.

- *Ludwig van Beethoven* (1770-1827) was deaf: "Though so deaf he could not hear the thunder for a token, he made music of his soul, the grandest ever spoken."

- *Alexander the Great* (356-323 BC) was a hunchback who became the king of Macedonia.

- *Sir Walter Scott* (1771-1832), though crippled, became a famous English author.

- *Francis Mouthelon*, who was awarded the 1000-franc prize by

139

the French society of artists for the loveliest painting in 1895, had no hands. He painted with wonderful skill by means of a wooden hand.

It is a fact that troubles often reveal heroes. It is the crisis that brings the best out in a person and often propels him to fame. People are not noted for their day-to-day existence but for the expert way they handle a storm. The winners are those who overcome problematic circumstances and refuse to be beaten by the invasion of difficulty into their lives.

> *Skilful pilots gain their reputation from storms and tempests.*
> — EPICURUS (341-270 BC)
> Greek philosopher

Strenuous and demanding situations call for strength not used on ordinary days. The grueling moments of the trial cause the soul to be strengthened. The tough things of life only make the winners tougher. Nothing can defeat them! They merely come out better and wiser.

> *Out of suffering have emerged the strongest souls.*
> — EDWIN HUBBEL CHAPIN (1814-1880)
> Clergyman and orator

Enrico Caruso, the great singer, had a favorite expression: *"Bisogna soffrire per essere grandi."* The words mean: "To be great, it is necessary to suffer." After years of difficulty, Caruso achieved fame, but the man communicated more than beautiful music through his voice. A music critic once observed, "His is a voice that loves you, but not only a voice, but a sympathetic man."

His trials gave him more sympathetic with the common people. This emotion was transferred to every listener. His singing became richer because of his suffering. His story told elsewhere in this book shares that his teacher told him he could not sing, but Caruso refused to give up his dream. It was not an easy road for him, but he was not after ease. He was following an ambition.

> *History has demonstrated that the most notable winners usually encountered heartbreaking obstacles before they triumphed. They won because they refused to become discouraged by their defeats.*
> — B. C. FORBES

Whatever life hands someone, it is his choice to determine

what he does with what has been dispensed to him. He can build, become, and triumph, or he can protest, excuse, and cave in to the pressure. "It takes a little courage and a little self-control and some grim determination if you want to reach a goal."[135]

We can throw stones, complain about them, stumble on them, climb over them, or build with them.
— WILLIAM ARTHUR WARD

The choice is either to collapse or to take courage, to build or to bawl, to capitulate or to capture. Victory is there but not without a price. When all is dark and totally beyond your ability to do anything positive about a situation, that is the time to forge ahead in spite of the circumstances! It takes courage to go forward in the face of defeat, to regain honor in the face of dishonor, or to believe when everything dictates failure.

Whether you be man or woman you will never do anything in this world without courage. It is the greatest quality of the mind next to honor.
— JAMES L. ALLEN

Mankind was not promised easy roads and painless advances but just the opposite. Life calls for courage in the face of danger, bravery when the situation calls for cowardice, strength when weakness invites, and sheer guts when everything fails. President Theodore Roosevelt once said: "It is only through labor and painful effort, by grim energy and resolute courage that we move to better things."

To move ahead when the deadly bullets of life are flying every which way takes nerve and valor. Those who wish to taste the sweetness of victory know that there is no place to stop until it is attained. Yes, even when the pressure is unbearable, energy is replaced with weariness, and the pain becomes excruciating, winners know to keep advancing. To vacillate is to lose.

When the morning's freshness has been replaced by the weariness of midday, when the leg muscles quiver under the strain, the climb seems endless, and, suddenly, nothing will go quite as you wish — it is then that you must not hesitate.
— DAG HAMMARSKJOLD (1905-1961)
Secretary General of the United Nations (1953-1961)

141

A scientist once said of Thomas A. Edison, "This poor fellow is wasting his time. Two fundamental laws of physics prove that he is attempting the impossible. The first is that there can be no light without combustion; the second is that no combustion can take place in a vacuum. Therefore, no light can be made in a vacuum." But even in the face of these *impossibilities,* Edison went right ahead and perfected the incandescent electric lamp. It was Cicero that said one of the mistakes of man was, "Insisting that a thing is impossible because we cannot accomplish it."[136]

"When Harvey insisted that blood flowed through the body, he was scoffed at. Pasteur's theories of germ life were scorned. Langley's plans for a machine which would fly without the help of a balloon were ridiculed. Even today, the man who is five years ahead of his time is looked upon as being a trifle balmy. The progress of the world depends upon men with vision and the courage to make their dreams come true."[137]

Courage is the power of being mastered by and possessed with an idea.

—PHILLIPS BROOKS (1835-1893)
American clergyman and bishop He is best remembered for his Christmas carol, "O Little Town of Bethlehem."

When circumstances dictate for one to retreat, that is often the time to advance! Instead of treading in fear, go forth in confidence with a dare. Dare to win and to overcome instead of feeling disenchanted and disillusioned. Rise and run into your dream with hope ablaze, reaching for that which appears out of reach.

Don't be afraid to take big steps. You can't cross a chasm in two small jumps.

—DAVID LLOYD GEORGE (1863-1945)
English statesman

A chasm can be the void in a life, an abyss of heartache and pain that threatens to destroy. Walking in fear, looking into the dark hole of failure or despair, does not require much doing. It is the brave soul, who chooses to take the big steps toward reaching a goal, that will be lifted into a realm of fulfillment and advancement. It is not an easy thing to do, but it necessitates steadfast effort and determination to go forward when everything else screams, "Give up!"

*We must not permit present problems to form a wall of bewil-
derment that shuts off our view of great futures.*
— DWIGHT D. EISENHOWER

No matter what happens, how great the obstacle is, how dark
the night, keep pushing forward. Triumph and victory will come, but
many times they will be after a fight. Fight on; fight on no matter how
hard the fight, for those who win fight on until victory comes!

*I wish to preach, not the doctrine of ignoble ease, but the doctrine of
the strenuous life, the life of toil and effort, of labor and strife; to
preach that the highest form of success which comes, not to the man
who desires mere easy peace, but to the man who does not shrink from
danger, from hardship, or from bitter toil, and who out of these wins
the splendid ultimate triumph.*
— THEODORE ROOSEVELT (1858-1919)

Before the triumph, during the times of struggle and hardship,
often it is necessary to overcome doubts and fears. Fear paralyzes
the mind and keeps one from thinking clearly. When there is fear,
there are torment and self-doubt, which restrict advance. If fear is
not conquered and is left to rule, it will dictate failure.

*If a man harbor any sort of fear, it percolates through all his think-
ing, damages his personality, makes him landlord to a ghost.*
— LLOYD CASSEL DOUGLAS (1877-1951)
Protestant minister, famous for his best-selling novels *Magnificent Obsession* (1929) *The Robe* (1942)

Fear keeps people from moving ahead, afraid to venture forth
toward new horizons. As they huddle in their safe, immobile positions, they tremble and cower even more. It is better to be on the offensive, going forward, tackling that which causes the fears, than it
is to wait trembling in the shadows for the worst to happen.

*Our doubts are traitors, and make us lose the good we oft might win,
by fearing to attempt.*
— SHAKESPEARE

One army lieutenant found a solution to his problem, as have
many others through the history of time. They have found that they
are never alone and that God is watching over them; therefore, their
faith is in Him as they learn to follow His guidance. Those that trust
in God can walk unafraid knowing that He is in complete control.

With Him in control, all is well, for He does all things well no matter how bad the situation is! It is simply a childlike faith in God.

My faith in God is complete, so I am unafraid.
— WILLIAM G. FARROW (1982-1942)
First Lieutenant United States Army Air Corps

Proverbs 3:5-6 simply states: "Trust in the LORD with all thine heart, and lean not unto thine own understanding. In all thy ways acknowledge him, and he shall direct thy paths." This is a promise! To be directed by God is success!

Faith in God is the cornerstone to true success. Without God, no success is lasting. "Faith always takes the first step forward. It is a soul sense, a spiritual foresight, which peers far beyond the physical eye's vision, a courier which leads the way, opens the closed door, sees beyond the obstacles, and points to the path which the less spiritual faculties could not see."[138]

Personal fears and doubts are not always what one must overcome, but there are times when it must be proven to those who are skeptical that their fears and skepticism were in vain. Some of the better-known incidents that bear this out are listed below:

- Benjamin Franklin's mother-in-law hesitated at letting her daughter marry a printer. There were already two printing offices in the United States, and she feared that the country might not be able to support a third.[139]

- A six-year-old lad came home with a note from his teacher in which it was suggested that he be taken out of school, as he was "too stupid to learn." That boy was Thomas A. Edison.

- Alfred Tennyson's grandfather gave him ten shillings for writing the eulogy on his grandmother. Handing it to the lad, the old man said: "There, that is the first money you ever earned by your poetry, and take my word for it, it will be the last."

- A boy was so slow to learn to talk that his parents thought him abnormal and his teachers called him a "misfit." His classmates avoided him and seldom invited him to play with them. He failed his first college entrance exam at a college in Zurich, Switzerland. A year later he tried again. In time he became world famous as a scientist. His name: Albert Einstein.

The main thing is for each individual to have convictions that he or she follows no matter what the climate around that one may be. There will always be those who do not believe. There will always be fears and doubts, but those who go forward bravely in spite of the fears and doubts are the true winners. President Theodore Roosevelt once said, "To do right at all times, in all places, and under all conditions, may take courage, but it pays, for the world is always looking for moral heroes to fill its high places."[140] One of those heroes was General Douglas MacArthur.

Moral courage is the courage of one's convictions, the courage to see things through. The world is in a constant conspiracy against the brave. It's the age-old struggle – the roar of the crowd on one side and the voice of your conscience on the other.
— DOUGLAS MAC ARTHUR (1880-1964)[141]
Famous American general of World War II

SUCCESS STORY:

NANCY MERKI

One of the most amazing stories of sheer courage in the face of tremendous odds is that of Nancy Merki. Stricken with polio at ten, she was condemned to wear heavy braces and later crutches. Yet in four years she became a swimming champion who told President Roosevelt, when he asked her how she had become the youngest champ despite infantile paralysis: "Well, I guess I just kept trying, Mr. President."

Her parents had taken her to a man named Jack Cody, swimming coach at an athletic club in Portland. It took a year to teach her to swim the length of the pool, but she was determined. Finally the coach realized that this young girl was not only interested in swimming as a means of restoring her health and the use of her limbs, but she wanted to be a champion. Four years after her paralytic attack, she came in third at a meet in Santa Barbara, California. At the age of nineteen, she changed her style of swimming and emerged from the meet as national champion. She just kept trying. Her handicaps, fears, and even the doubts of others did not hold her back. Obstacles that would have stopped many only spurred Nancy on to victory!

145

SUCCESS NUGGETS:

BUILDING

Upon the wreckage of thy yesterday
Design the structure of tomorrow.
Lay strong cornerstones of purpose, and prepare
Great blocks of wisdom cut from past despair
Shape mighty pillars of resolve,
To set deep in the tear-wet mortar of regret.
Believe in God — in thine own self believe
All thou hast hoped for thou shalt yet achieve.
— ELLA WHEELER WILCOX[142]

Difficulties are absolutely nothing to the man who knows that he is on the mission on which God has sent him. They are only opportunities for him to show his power; problems to manifest his skill in their solution; thunderclouds on which to paint the frescoes of his unrealized tenderness.
— REV. F. B. MEYER[143]

If you'll simply go after that thing that you want,
With all your capacity,
Strength and sagacity,
Faith, hope and confidence, stern pertinacity,
If neither cold poverty, famished and gaunt,
Nor sickness nor pain
Of body and brain
Can turn you away from the thing that you want,
If dogged and grim you besiege and beset it,
    You'll get it.
— BERTON BRALEY[144]

13
GIVE THE BEST AND EXPECT THE BEST

"Give, and it shall be given you; good measure, pressed down, and shaken together, and running over, shall men give into your bosom. For with the same measure that ye mete withal it shall be measured to you again" (Luke 6:38).

Proverbs 11:25 says it well: "The liberal soul shall be made fat: and he that watereth shall be watered also himself." They who give liberally shall have much given back to them. They shall be made rich and blessed in the things that count. If one gives the best, the best shall come back to him. Ecclesiastes 11:1 states, "Cast thy bread upon the waters: for thou shalt find it after many days." It shall come back!

It is a funny thing about life; if you refuse to accept anything but the best, you very often get it.
— W. SOMERSET MAUGHAM (1875-1965)
British author

I do the very best I know how — the very best I can; and I mean to keep doing so.
— ABRAHAM LINCOLN

The best: what is it? It is the finest there is, nothing second-rate, shoddy, or inferior. It is the cream off the top; it is excellence instead of mediocrity. The best is the optimum quality available. One line of an old song affirms this: "Give to the world the best you have and the best will come back to you." The following poem captures the truth of this song.

MY WAGE
I bargained with Life for a penny,
And Life would pay no more,
However I begged at evening
When I counted my scanty store;

For Life is a just employer,
He gives you what you ask,
But once you have set the wages,
Why, you must bear the task.

I worked for a menial's hire,
Only to learn, dismayed,
That any wage I had asked of Life,
Life would have paid.
— JESSIE B. RITTENHOUSE (1869-1948)[145]
American poet

People choose what they give life. Every day is a blank page waiting to be filled with the actions and events of the day. On that page will be recorded the attitudes displayed, decisions made, and the quality given to each moment. Each person's page will be written by himself, for he is the author of his life. What he is, what he does, and how the day was spent are documented each evening. So the best thing a person can do for himself is to live each day well.

The best preparation for tomorrow is to do today's work superbly well.
— SIR WILLIAM OSLER (1849-1919)
Canadian physician and brilliant medical teacher

The best does not just happen, but conscious effort must be made in order to attain it. Resolute determination to make the right choice, to have the proper attitude, to give the best must be realized in a competent manner.

"Quality is never an accident; it is always the result of high intention, sincere effort, intelligent direction and skillful execution; it represents the wise choice of many alternatives."
— WILLA A. FOSTER

The age-old maxim, *you reap what you sow*, is definitely true. Whatever is given out from any individual will come back to him, as depicted in the following poem:

LIFE'S MIRROR
There are loyal hearts, there are spirits brave,
    There are souls that are pure and true;
Then give to the world the best you have,
    And the best will come back to you.

Give love, and love to your life will flow,
    A strength in your utmost need;
Have faith, and a score of hearts will show
    Their faith in your word and deed.

Give truth, and your gift will be paid in kind,
    And honor will honor meet;
And a smile that is sweet will surely find
    A smile that is just as sweet.

Give sorrow and pity to those who mourn;
    You will gather in flowers again
The scattered seeds of your thoughts outborne,
    Though the sowing seemed but vain.

For life is the mirror of king and slave—
    'Tis just what we are and do;
Then give to the world the best you have,
    And the best will come back to you.
                    — MADELINE BRIDGES[146]
                    Writer of American poetry (1844-1920)

There is something adventurous in trying to bring the best into everything that is done. Life becomes a work of art, and all actions act as the paint for the canvas each day. Every person is the artist of his own life's painting. To paint well means that effort is applied in

149

everything that is done. It is to realize that each moment is important and worthwhile, and what is brought into that moment helps color the rest of the day and even a life.

> *The pleasure resulting from work well done is worthwhile. To develop the best equipped railroad, to conduct the most successful bank, to create a great store where principle never yields to mere money making, to create an environment for the young man or woman just entering a business career that will be an incentive to do greater things, become a pleasure and remuneration far beyond any money value. It is as great a thing to develop merchandise of character and beauty as to paint a fine picture, carve a beautiful statue, or write a good book. To some manufacturers a carpet is just a carpet, a piece of gingham is only a piece of gingham. But with the desire to make the best – carpet or a piece of gingham can become a work of art.*
> — JOHN G. SHEDD (1850-1926)
> Merchant and philanthropist, chosen president of Marshall Field & Co. in 1906

Achieving excellence is not an accident but a purpose fulfilled. To do things superbly, not half-heartedly, should be the goal of the winner. Excellence should be a lifestyle that manifests itself in fineness and quality in all that is done. It is not an afterthought but something premeditated. There should be planning and forethought in each act of the day until quality and excellence become the norm.

> *We are what we repeatedly do. Excellence, then, is not an act, but a habit.*
> — ARISTOTLE

Martin Luther King, Jr., adhered to this philosophy and walked in excellence even when he was misunderstood by those who opposed him. He did not let nastiness creep into his lifestyle or attitudes even though he rubbed shoulders with those who manifested hate and intolerance. He is famous for the following speech that eulogizes excellence:

> *We are challenged on every hand to work untiringly to achieve excellence in our lifework. Not all men are called to specialized or professional jobs; even fewer rise to the heights of genius in the arts and sciences; many are called to be laborers in factories, fields, and streets.*

But no work is insignificant. All labor that uplifts humanity has dignity and importance and should be undertaken with painstaking excellence. If a man is called to be a street sweeper, he should sweep even as Michelangelo painted, or Beethoven composed music, or Shakespeare wrote poetry. He should sweep streets so well that all the host of heaven and earth will pause to say, "Here lived a great street sweeper who did his job well."

— MARTIN LUTHER KING, JR. (1929-1968)
American minister, civil rights activist, and writer

If, at the end of every day, a person can say, "I have done my best," then that person will live well. To be able to achieve excellence and to give oneself to such a goal are premium. To contribute something worthwhile to a cause, and to throw oneself into it with fervor and quality of service are things to be lauded. It is not only the cause that advances, but the person who initiated the cause is the one who receives the most reward.

Helen Keller once wrote, "When we do the best we can, we never know what miracle is wrought in our own life or in the life of another."[147]

And as you advance, ask: "What have I done for my country?" And this you will do until the moment when you may experience the supreme happiness of thinking that you have in some way contributed to progress and the good of humanity. But to whatever degree life will have favored your efforts, when you approach the great goal, you must be able to say to yourself: "I have done my best."

— LOUIS PASTEUR[148]

SUCCESS STORY:

EDWARD ROWLAND SILL

Edward Rowland Sill was born in Windsor, Connecticut, on April 29, 1841, and was orphaned at a very young age. His health was poor and he could not do many things he would have liked to do, but he was allowed to spend summers with his uncle, Elisha Sill, an early settler of Cuyahoga Falls.

Edward determined to get an education and graduated from Yale in 1861. For a long time he had difficulty finding his proper niche in life and tried different things. In 1867 he attended Divinity school at Harvard, but soon left there not feeling suited to this type

151

of work. He then decided on a career in education. He had many setbacks, but he believed in doing the best he could with what he had no matter what the condition in which he found himself.

He taught in Wadsworth, Ohio, and Cuyahoga Falls, but ill health prompted him to move to California. While there he served as English literature chairman at the University of California from 1874 to 1882. His philosophy by which he had lived and which he had always tried to teach others: "We must do the best we can with what we have."

This idea is beautifully symbolized in the following poem, which is one of his most famous writings:

OPPORTUNITY
This I beheld, or dreamed it in a dream:
There spread a cloud of dust along a plain:
And underneath the cloud, or in it, raged
A furious battle, and men yelled, and swords
Shocked upon swords and shields. A prince's banner
Wavered, then staggered backward, hemmed by foes.
A craven hung along the battle's edge
And thought, "Had I a sword of keener steel—
That blue blade that the king's son bears—but this
Blunt thing—!" He snapt and flung it from his hand,
And, lowering, crept away and left the field.
Then came the king's son, wounded, sore bestead,
And weaponless, and saw the broken sword,
Hilt-buried in the dry and trodden sand,
And ran and snatched it, and with battle-shout
Lifted afresh, he hewed his enemy down,
And saved a great cause that heroic day.[149]

SUCCESS NUGGETS:
Whatever I have tried to do in life, I have tried with all my heart to do well; whatever I have devoted myself to, I have devoted myself to completely; in great aims and in small, I have always been thoroughly in earnest.
—DICKENS[150]

To do the best thing possible, to you, it is just as necessary to get yourself in tune for the day, in tune with the best things in you, as it is for musicians in an orchestra to get in tune, into harmony with the keynote of what they are going to play.[151]

This Is Success

To live well. To laugh often. To love much. To gain the respect of intelligent men.

To win the love of little children.

To fill one's niche and accomplish one's task.

To leave the world better than one finds it, whether by an improved flower, a perfect poem or another life ennobled.

To never lack appreciation of earth's beauty or fail to express it.

To always look for the best in others.

To give the best one has.

To make one's life an inspiration and one's memory a benediction.[152]

14

IMPROVE YOURSELF
AND DEVELOP
GOOD CHARACTER

"For in him we live, and move, and have our being; as certain also of your own poets have said, For we are also his offspring" (Acts 17:28).

We were created in God's image. He wants us to walk in integrity and to become what we were created to be. We owe it to ourselves to develop good character, to be honest, and to work at improving ourselves. The greatest thing we can do in life is to please God! To have His approval and have Him work with us is the ultimate!

It is our privilege and duty to: "Live the strong life. Keep right with God. Be an overcomer. Think great thoughts. Be strong. Think thoughts of strength, beauty, love, and courage and the power of a fine personality will grow and develop."[153]

Integrity will guide a person as stated in Proverbs 11:3: "The integrity of the upright shall guide them." The first president of the United States based his life and presidency on one of the qualities of good character; that of integrity, shown in the following quote:

Integrity and firmness are all I can promise. These, be the voyage long or short, shall never forsake me, although I may be deserted by

Improve Yourself and Develop Good Character

all men; for of the consolations, which are to be derived from these, under any circumstances, the world cannot deprive me.
— GEORGE WASHINGTON (1732-1799)[154]
This statement was in a letter written April 1, 1739, to Henry Knox four weeks prior to assuming the Presidency.

Proverbs 19:5: states what happens to those without integrity: "A false witness shall not be unpunished, and he that speaketh lies shall not escape."

Every person who seeks to be successful should seek to be truthful and honest. Integrity is as pure gold, but it cannot be bought! No matter the state of a person as of right now, anyone can seek to have integrity and improve their character; it can be attained.

To improve is to make something better, to make progress, or to advance instead of retreating. There are deposited into every life bitter experiences that should only sharpen and shape the character into something more magnificent. Sadly, there are some souls who, when situations invade their world that have the potential of building character, wither, when the case should be just the opposite: a blooming should take place. True success can never be achieved without the scalding hurts and disappointments that force their way into each of our lives.

Character cannot be developed in ease and quiet. Only through experiences of trial and suffering can the soul be strengthened, vision cleared, ambition inspired and success achieved.
— HELEN KELLER

The best things often come when a soul has come face to face with setbacks and defeats. They are the very things that help sharpen the senses and remove confusion. Without them life would be one long party, and people would become soft, lazy, and unfulfilled. To push against an obstacle strengthens the soul.

During the interval of pressure and struggle, this is the time to look at those who have improved during their struggles. It has been said that people are in competition with themselves, and that is fine if the person keeps pressing toward betterment but often this is not the case. He becomes satisfied with less because he has no one to look to inspire him to greater things.

People seldom improve when they have no other model but themselves to copy after.
— OLIVER GOLDSMITH (1728-1774)
British poet, playwright, and novelist

156

When anyone becomes discontent with self, it is essential for that one to understand it is time for self-improvement and a strengthening of inward character. This should be done with a healthy outlook and not the sickness of the ultra perfectionist, in which things can never be right and the person can never be content. We can accept our limitations if they are not self-imposed, but we should never accept bad character.

Blessed is the man who, seeing his own face as in a mirror and haunted with a divine discontent at the manner of man he is, goes on to perfection.
— AUTHOR UNKNOWN

Hold back nothing in your quest for good character and self-improvement, for the very core of life consists of what a person is, does, and thinks. These determine everything about a person and the quality of life he or she enjoys. The largeness of eternity should beckon us to greater things, and the miracle of life should not be wasted but lived to the maximum.

Bad will be the day for every man when he becomes absolutely contented with the life that he is living, with the thoughts that he is thinking, with the deeds that he is doing, when there is not forever beating at the doors of his soul some great desire to do something larger, which he knows that he was meant and made to do because he is still, in spite of all, the child of God.
— PHILLIPS BROOKS[155]

To be rich is to be full of good character or working to attain it. Temporal riches without character are in vain. They only lead to dissatisfaction and emptiness. True riches reside inside a person. This is what colors our world and our everyday lives.

There is nothing that makes men rich and strong but that which they carry inside of them. Wealth is of the heart, not of the hand.
— JOHN MILTON

It is not enough to have ability and talent; these can only elevate a person so far. What makes people act the way they do is what is important. That is the root cause of the matter. As someone once said so ably:

157

Ability may get you to the top, but only character will keep you there!
— AUTHOR UNKNOWN

Principles are important and are the very fiber of life! People cannot act any way they please and expect to reap a harvest of good things. Careful daily planting of good deeds based on a code of ethics will harvest bountiful rewards. Morality is essential to help foster good, healthy relationships throughout society, in the work place, and in the home. Theodore Roosevelt said, "To do right at all times, in all places, and under all conditions, may take courage, but it pays, for the world is always looking for moral heroes to fill its high places."[156]

General principles . . . are to the facts as the root and sap of a tree [are] to its leaves.
— SAMUEL TAYLOR COLERIDGE (1772-1834)
English poet, essayist, and critic

The struggle to have and to apply and enforce good principles in everyday life is a challenge but must be done for healthy growth. Years ago someone wrote the following, which still applies in today's world:

THE SEVEN MODERN SINS

Polices without principles
Pleasure without conscience
Wealth without work
Knowledge without character
Industry without morality
Science without humanity
Worship without sacrifice.
— AUTHOR UNKNOWN

The famous author, Leo Tolstoy, once penned the words that in many instances are true. They are as follows:

Everyone thinks of changing the world, but no one thinks of changing himself.
— LEO TOLSTOY (1828-1910)
One of Russia's most celebrated writers of fiction

Tolstoy was also an important moral thinker and a social reformer. Tolstoy wrote *War and Peace* (1865-1869), "which was perhaps the greatest work in the whole range of Russian realistic fiction, and *Anna Karenina* (1875-1877), one of the great love stories of the world."

Tolstoy's parents died when he was a boy, and he was brought up by relatives. As a youth, Tolstoy had often pondered over difficult questions concerning the meaning and purpose of life. At the age of forty-six, seemingly happy, prosperous, and famous, these questions bothered him so much that he felt he must try to find a solution to them.

He read widely in religious and philosophical books and talked and corresponded with many wise men for several years. He then believed he had found an explanation to life's meaning in the true significance of Christ's preaching "to resist not evil." Tolstoy believed that every man had within himself the power to understand what is good and that man would justify his life on earth by striving to do good for himself and others. He condemned all violence, gave up tobacco and intoxicating liquors, and became a vegetarian. He dressed simply, worked in the fields with the peasants, and tried to be as self-sufficient as possible. He preached charity and helped others in distress. He insisted that society would become better only when all men and women tried to become more perfect in their personal lives and learned to love each other. His unusual views and principles and his way of life often brought him into conflict with the government and even with his own family.

Tolstoy, as many others, was in search of making the world a better place. His summation that society would become better only when all men and women try to become more perfect in their personal lives and learn to love one another is foreign to many people. As some have said, "It's a dog eat dog world out there." The question is, "Do we allow the world situations to dictate to us how to act, or do we form our own set of actions based on a higher authority, the Holy Bible?"

People cannot operate according to their own intellect but must be guided by the "divine fire" of inspiration. Each of us is one person, but together we make a whole; therefore, it is important to make the best of ourselves because we are a part of one another.

Make the most of yourself, for that is all there is of you.
— RALPH WALDO EMERSON

Often when someone is trying to make the best of his life, he comes under attack and is criticized. But criticism can be a friend.

Improve Yourself and Develop Good Character

Dale Carnegie told the following story that proves this:

> *I know a former soap salesman who used to even to ask for criticism. When he first started out selling soap for Colgate, orders came slowly. He worried about losing his job. Since he knew there was nothing wrong with the soap or the price, he figured that the trouble must be himself. When he failed to make a sale, he would often walk around the block trying to figure out what was wrong. Had he been too vague? Did he lack enthusiasm? Sometimes he would go back to the merchant and say: "I haven't come back here to try to sell you any soap. I have come back to get your advice and your criticism. Won't you please tell me what I did that was wrong when I tried to sell you soap a few minutes ago? You are far more experienced and successful than I am. Please give me your criticism. Be frank. Don't pull your punches."*[157]

This attitude won him a lot of friends and priceless advice. He eventually became the president of the Colgate-Palmolive Soap Company — one of the world's largest makers of soap. His name was E. H. Little.

So when the criticism comes, examine it for what it is, then cull the good, throw away that which is based on jealousy and meanness, and continue in the quest of being the best you can be. It is not easy to rise higher when the beds of ease beckon. It is a fight.

The toughest wars are not fought on the battlefields, but they are fought inside the heart of a man or woman. It is easy to read and thus be inspired to live better lives, but the real battle begins when the heat of life is applied to everyday living. To change habits that erode character is not an easy thing to do, but it is possible for those who choose to fight for what is right.

> *Who has a fiercer struggle than he who strives to conquer himself?*
> — THOMAS A. KEMPIS (1380-1471)
> German author

Dare to be right! Dare to be true!
You have a work that no other can do;
Do it so bravely, so kindly, so well,
Angels will hasten the story to tell.
Dare to be right! Dare to be true!
The failings of others can never save you;

Stand by your conscience, your honor, your faith,
Stand like a hero, and battle till death![158]

Whatever happens, dare to be right and true! It does not matter if you have failed in the struggle, whether it is once, twice, or many times. The thing that matters is to be right inside of you, as you struggle to never give up. To compromise one's ideals in order to "make it" is to die a worse death in the end. You simply must stay true to truth and God's principles in order to succeed His way! It is not enough to succeed by man's standards; God's standards are the criteria for success. So stand tall and be brave in this journey called life, but never give up following the dreams God has placed in your heart! Let your conscience talk to you; don't squelch it or put a blanket over your inner ears, but listen carefully for it is a gift from God!

So in the midst of a world gone crazy, dare to be right! Dare to be true! For this is the only way to live successfully. Any other way is a sham and in the end will be empty success.

You can become and be, as the following author penned so beautifully:

NO STAR IS EVER LOST
Have we not all, amid life's petty strife,
Some pure ideal of a noble life
That once seemed possible? Did we not hear
The flutter of its wings and feel it near,
And just within our reach? It was. And yet

We lost it in this daily jar and fret.
But still our place is kept and it will wait,
Ready for us to fill it, soon or late.
No star is ever lost we once have seen:
We always may be what we might have been.[159]
— ADELAIDE DELIDE A. PROCTER (1825-1864)
English poetess

To conquer self is a great feat! It comes by the daily application of knowledge and combining good character with every transaction. To be what we might be is within our grasp, but it takes effort and perseverance to do so.

To live without shame, to walk without guilt, to treat others respectfully and live each moment well are to achieve success. If

only everyone would do what the famous Will Rogers so humor-
ously said to do.

> *Lead your life so you wouldn't be ashamed to sell the family parrot*
> *to the town gossip.*
> — WILL ROGERS (1879-1935)
> American humorist and author

Truth comes as an inner light that shines into the crevices of
our heart and mind. Enlightenment comes, and then the time comes
for the choice to be made: Either improve or continue in the same
dark path that leads on a downward spiral toward failure and defeat. Truth is given to improve. It is not given to crush or put down,
but is given to lift one up into a greater realm of living. What we do
with it determines our destiny.

> *Men occasionally stumble over the truth, but most of them pick them-*
> *selves up and hurry off as if nothing happened.*
> — WINSTON CHURCHILL (1874-1965).

SUCCESS STORY:

WINSTON CHURCHILL

Churchill became one of the greatest statesmen in world history. He was also a noted speaker, author, painter, soldier, and war
reporter. Early in World War II, Britain stood alone against Nazi
Germany. The British refused to give in despite the huge odds
against them. Churchill's personal courage, the magic of his words,
and his faith in victory inspired the British to "their finest hour."
The mere sight of this stocky, determined man, with two fingers
raised high in a "V for Victory" salute, cheered the people.

Churchill not only made history, he also wrote it. As a histo-
rian, war reporter, and biographer, he showed a matchless command of the English language. In 1953, he won the Nobel Prize for
literature. Yet as a schoolboy, he had been the worst student in the
class. Churchill spoke as he wrote—clearly, vividly, majestically. Yet
he had stuttered as a boy.

He entered the service of his country in 1895 as an army lieutenant under Queen Victoria. He ended his career in 1964 as a member of the House of Commons under Queen Elizabeth II, the
great-great-granddaughter of Queen Victoria. Few men ever served

their country so long or so well. He became Prime Minister in 1940 and retired as Prime Minister in 1955.

Young Winston, a chunky lad with a mop of red hair, had an unhappy boyhood. He talked with a stutter and lisp and did poorly in his schoolwork. His teacher's report reads: "The boy is certainly no scholar and has repeated his grade twice. He has also a stubborn streak and is sometimes rebellious in nature. He seems to have little or no understanding of his schoolwork, except in a most mechanical way. At times, he seems almost perverse in his ability to learn. He has not made the most of his opportunities."[160] His stubbornness and high spirits annoyed everyone. In addition, his parents had little time for him.

Truth came to him concerning the war. As he mulled it over, it pounded in his brain until he spoke it to a fragile nation days immediately after Dunkirk, which were darkest for the modern world. England lay prostrate. Forty-seven warships had been sunk in the operations off Norway after Dunkirk. When the evacuation was completed, half the British destroyers were in the shipyards for repairs while the Royal Air Force had lost 40 percent of its bomber strength. Britain was on the brink of famine, and her armies were without arms or equipment. They had left in France fifty thousand vehicles.

Churchill spoke: "We shall defend our island whatever the cost may be; we shall fight on the beaches; we shall fight in the fields; we shall fight in the streets; and we shall fight in the hill. We shall never surrender and if this island were subjugated and starving, our empire on the seas would carry on the struggle until in God's good time the New World with all its power and might steps forth to the rescue and liberation of the old."[161]

The following is an excerpt from a speech Churchill made to the House of Commons on March 28, 1950:

Man in this moment of his history has emerged in greater supremacy over the forces of nature than has ever been dreamed of before. He has it in his power to solve quite easily the problems of material existence. He has conquered the wild beasts, and he has even conquered the insect and microbes. There lies before him, as he wishes, a golden age of peace and progress. All is in his hand. He has only to conquer his last and worst enemy — himself. With vision, faith and courage, it may be within our power to win a crowning victory for all.

SUCCESS NUGGETS:

Character is the result of the cultivation of the highest and noblest qualities in human nature, and putting these qualities to practical use.
— ELLA WHEELER WILCOX[162]

You cannot dream yourself into a character. You must hammer and forge yourself one.
— JAMES ANTHONY FROUDE[163]

Life is not mere length of time, but the daily web of character we unconsciously weave. Our thoughts, imaginations, purposes, motives, love, will, are the under threads: our words, tone of voice, looks, acts, habits are the upper threads: and the passing moment is the shuttle swiftly, ceaselessly, relentlessly, weaving those threads into a web, and that web is life. It is woven, not by our wishing, or willing, but irresistible, unavoidable, woven by what we are, moment by moment, hour after hour.[164]

Every man is the builder of a temple called his body. . . . We are all sculptors and painters, and our material is our own flesh and blood and bones. Any nobleness begins at once to refine a man's features, any meanness or sensuality to imbrute them.
— HENRY DAVID THOREAU[165]

Character is more than intellect. A great soul will be strong to live, as well as to think. Goodness outshines genius, as the sun makes the electric light cast a shadow.
— EMERSON[166]

Character is destiny.   — HERACLITUS
Character is power.   — BOOKER WASHINGTON

15
ENTHUSIASM WORKS WONDERS

"These that have turned the world upside down are come hither also" (Acts 17:6).

The early church was on fire with enthusiasm with the doctrine of Jesus Christ. So great was their fire that they were known to literally turn everything and every place upside down from its normal operations.

Merriam-Webster's Collegiate Dictionary-Eleventh Edition defines enthusiasm as belief in special revelations of the Holy Spirit, a strong excitement of feeling, something inspiring zeal or fervor.

Enthusiasm is the greatest business asset in the world. It beats money and power and influence. Single-handed the enthusiast convinces and dominates where a small army of workers would scarcely raise a tremor of interest.

Enthusiasm tramples over prejudice and opposition, spurns inaction, storms the citadel of its object, and like an avalanche overwhelms and engulfs all obstacles.

Enthusiasm is faith in action; and faith and initiative rightly combined remove mountainous barriers and achieve the unheard of and miraculous.

Set the germ of enthusiasm afloat in your business, carry it in your attitude and manner; it spreads like a contagion and influences every fiber of your industry; it begets and inspires effects you did not dream of.

It means increase in production and decrease in costs; it means joy and pleasure and satisfaction to your workers; it means like real and virile; it means spontaneous bedrock results — the vital things that pay dividends.

—ELECTROCRAFT[167]

To be enthused is to be inspired and motivated. An enthusiast is one who is ardently attached to a cause, object, or pursuit. The opposite of enthusiasm is apathy. Hum-ho, deadness, boredom do not describe enthusiasm. When a person is enthused, there is an eagerness, passion, zeal, and keen interest in something.

Dean C. Dutton, PhD, states: "Enthusiasm is the driving power of the soul. It is steam up. It is the basis of earnestness. It is the urge of endeavor. It is the life of that tenacity of purpose that pushes a thing through to success. When enthusiasm is gone the engine is dead. Failure has come. But a never failing enthusiasm—who can measure its inestimable value! So this matter of a mighty enthusiasm is not only a study of gladness; it is the very vital matter of success. If we can find how to sustain a great enthusiasm no matter what the material surroundings then we have found a most important source of power—the very key to all success."[168]

A man can succeed at almost anything for which he has unlimited enthusiasm.

— CHARLES SCHWAB (1862-1939)
Founder and president of both the United States Steel Corporation and Bethlehem Steel Corporation

Schwab started as an engineer's stake driver with the Carnegie Company. He rose rapidly and became the first president of United States Steel in 1901. Resigning in 1903, he took control of Bethlehem Steel Corporation and directed its growth in shipbuilding, munitions, and allied fields. His enthusiasm helped take him to the top of his field.

Wise Solomon of old wrote, "Whatsoever thy hand findeth to do, do it with thy might; for there is no work, nor device, nor knowledge, nor wisdom, in the grave, whither thou goest" (Ecclesiastes 9:10).

Whatever you are involved with, seek to do it wholeheartedly. Enthusiasm is like a fire of passion that warms every soul it touches.

It can help to light fires in the people around you. It is very catching; nothing is quite contagious as enthusiasm.

Often someone will say, "I don't feel enthusiastic." William James, the psychologist wrote, "Action seems to follow feeling, but really action and feeling go together; and by regulating the action, which is under the more direct control of the will, we can indirectly regulate the feeling, which is not."

Many people let their feelings dominate them. They live in ruts because they let their circumstances and surroundings put out their fire. They are half alive and half dead.

The only difference between a rut and a grave is their dimensions.
— ELLEN GLASGOW (1874-1945)
American author

Ellen wrote witty, compassionate novels about upper-class life in the South. Because she was a delicate child, she had little schooling. But she read widely in her father's large library. She struggled silently for intellectual independence. Her family hardly recognized her struggle, and when she finally revealed herself as the author of an anonymous novel, *The Descendant* (1897), they were as surprised as other people.

Anyone can be successful if he is passionate about what he does and is willing to crowbar himself out of the rut. Yes, it will take some effort and change of habits, but it can be accomplished. The first thing that needs to be done is to take a new look at what one is involved in, see the positive points of that venture, and then get a new love and excitement for what he or she is doing. Nothing can stop someone from succeeding when this happens, as one unknown author wrote, "Success comes to men who are in love with their work, who believe in it with all their soul, and who radiate their belief until it penetrates everyone around them."

If you want to do a great thing, you must be enthused and excited about it. The fire of that passion will keep you motivated and sustained through setbacks, hardships, and impossible odds.

Every great and commanding movement in the annals of the world is the triumph of enthusiasm. Nothing great was ever achieved without it.
— RALPH WALDO EMERSON

Watch a child who is busy trying to do something that is difficult to do, but his desire to do it is bigger than the challenge. His eyes shine with determination, and he is alive with enthusiasm. It is written all over his countenance. He will succeed given time. There is no true success without enthusiasm!

No one has success until he has the abounding life. This is made up of the many-fold activity of energy, enthusiasm and gladness. It is to spring to meet the day with a thrill at being alive. It is to go forth to meet the morning in an ecstasy of joy. It is to realize the oneness of humanity in true spiritual sympathy.[169]
— LILLIAN WHITING (1847-1942)
American journalist, essayist, poet, biographer, and editor

SUCCESS STORY:

FRANK BETTGER

Frank Bettger came up the hard way, received little formal education, and never finished grade school. His father died when he was just a small boy, leaving his mother with five little children. When he was eleven years old, he had to get up at four-thirty in the morning to sell newspapers on street corners to help his widowed mother, who took in washing and sewing in order to help feed her family.

At fourteen, he had to leave school and took a job as a steamfitter's helper. At eighteen, he became a professional baseball player, and for two years he played third base for the St. Louis Cardinals. Then one day in Chicago, Illinois, while playing against the Chicago Cubs, he injured his arm and was forced to give up baseball.

He went back to Philadelphia, his hometown, and became a salesman trying to sell life insurance. He was a total failure, but something happened that changed his life. He rose from a failure to one of the most successful salesmen in America. Enthusiasm took Frank Bettger out of the ranks of failure and helped transform him into one of the nation's highest paid salesmen. The following is his story:

Shortly after I started out as a professional baseball player, I got one of the biggest shocks of my life. That was back in 1907. I was playing for Johnstown, Pennsylvania, in the Tri-State League. I was young and ambitious — wanted to get to the top — and what hap-

pened? I was fired! . . . .The manager said he fired me because I was lazy! . . . "You drag yourself around the field like a veteran who has been playing ball for twenty years," he told me. "Why do you act that way if you're not lazy?"

"Well, Bert," I said, "I'm so nervous, so scared, that I want to hide my fear from the crowd, and especially from the other players on the team. Besides, I hope that by taking it easy, I'll get rid of my nervousness."

"Frank," he said, "it will never work. That's the thing that is holding you down. Whatever you do after you leave here, for heaven's sake, wake yourself up, and put some life and enthusiasm into you work!". . .

Danny Meehan induced New Haven, Connecticut, to give me a trial. I made up my mind to establish the reputation of being the most enthusiastic ball player they'd ever seen in the New England League. From the minute I appeared on the field, I acted like a man electrified. I acted as though I were alive with a million batteries. I threw the ball around the diamond so fast and so hard that it almost knocked our infielders' hands apart. . . . Yes, it was all a show, an act I was putting on. Did it work? It worked like magic. Two things happened:

1. *My enthusiasm almost entirely overcame my fear. In fact my nervousness began to work for me, and I played far better than I ever thought I was capable of playing.*

2. *My enthusiasm affected the other players on the team, and they too became enthusiastic.*

My biggest thrill came the following morning when I read in the New Haven newspaper: "This new player, Bettger, has a barrel of enthusiasm. He inspired our boys. They not only won the game, but looked better than at any time this season."[170]

After Bettger's accident, when he was forced to leave baseball and to become a salesman, he said,

The next ten months were the longest and most disheartening months of my life: a dismal failure at selling life insurance. I finally decided that I was never cut out to be a salesman, and began answering want ads for a job as a shipping clerk. . . . I realized that no matter what work I tried to do, I had to overcome a strange fear-complex that possessed me, so I joined one of Dale Carnegie's courses in public speaking. One night, Mr. Carnegie stopped me in the middle of a talk. "Mr. Bettger," he said, "just a moment. . . . Just a moment.

Are you interested in what you are saying?"
"Yes, of course I am," I replied.
"Well, then," said Mr. Carnegie, "why don't you talk with a little enthusiasm? How do you expect your audience to be interested if you don't put some life and animation into what you say?"
Before I went to bed that night, I sat for an hour thinking. My thoughts went back to my baseball days at Johnstown and New Haven. For the first time, I realized that the very fault, which had threatened to wreck my career in baseball, was now threatening to wreck my career as a salesman. The decision I made that night was the turning point of my life. That decision was to stay in the insurance business and put the same enthusiasm into selling that I had put into playing baseball when I joined the New Haven team.[171]

Bettger once read a statement by Walter P. Chrysler and was so impressed by it that he carried it in his pocked for a week. He said he read it over forty times, until he knew it by heart. Walter Chrysler, when asked to give the secret of success, listed the various qualities, such as ability, capacity, energy, but added that the real secret was enthusiasm. "Yes, more than enthusiasm," said Chrysler, "I would say excitement. I like to see men get excited. When they get excited, they get customers excited, and we get business."

Bettger concluded that, "Enthusiasm isn't merely an outward expression. Once you begin to acquire it, enthusiasm works constantly within you. You may be sitting quietly in your home . . . an idea occurs to you . . . that idea begins to develop, finally, you become consumed with enthusiasm . . . nothing can stop you."[172]

SUCCESS NUGGETS:

SUCCESS

SUCCESS! It's found in the soul of you,
And not in the realms of luck!
The world will furnish the work to do,
But you must provide the pluck.
You can do whatever you think you can,
It's all in the way you view it.
It's all in the start you make
You must feel that you're going to do it.
— EDGAR A. GUEST[173]

Nothing great was ever achieved without enthusiasm.
— RALPH WALDO EMERSON

Courage is going from failure to failure without losing enthusiasm.
— WINSTON CHURCHILL

It's faith in something and enthusiasm for something that makes life worth living.
— OLIVER WENDELL HOLMES

16
KEEP FOCUSED

"This one thing I do, forgetting those things which are behind, and reaching forth unto those things which are before"
(Philippians 3:13).

"This one thing I do": his thoughts were focused on one thing!
Thoughts are things! Focused thoughts will help launch a person into accomplishment. The person who has the ability to focus
will unleash success vibrations that send signals to everything he
touches. Everyone has the power to become something and to reach
his goals if he can rule his thoughts.

> *Our destiny changes with our thought; we shall become what we*
> *wish to become, do what we wish to do, when our habitual thought*
> *corresponds with our desire.*
> —ORISON S. MARDEN

Paul, the apostle, wrote: "Let this mind be in you, which was
also in Christ Jesus" (Philippians 2:5). The mind, the thinking
process is very powerful. What you allow yourself to think upon,
that is what you will become. Instruction is given in Philippians 4:8
as to what to think about: "Finally, brethren, whatsoever things are

true, whatsoever things are honest, whatsoever things are just, whatsoever things are pure, whatsoever things are lovely, whatsoever things are of good report; if there be any virtue, and if there be any praise, think on these things."

You are today where your thoughts have brought you; you will be tomorrow where your thoughts take you.
—JAMES ALLEN (1864-1912)
Gained fame as a novelist and poet. None of his many books received the lasting fame of *As a Man Thinketh*

There are people who allow themselves to go through life half-dead, leading a humdrum life, not really delving into the realm of thought that can lead to eternal things and greatness in God. They simply do not think. They just exist and are like a mass that receives messages from the thinker.

Most people would rather die than think: many do.
— BERTRAND RUSSELL (1872-1970)
British philosopher, logician, essayist, Nobel Prize winner for literature in 1950

Success starts in the mind. Thinking is the door that leads you into corridors of life and power. Harness good thoughts, but obliterate bad or negative producing thoughts.

THINK
If you think you are beaten, you are;
If you think you dare not, you don't;
If you'd like to win, but think you can't,
It's almost a cinch you won't.

If you think you'll lose, you're lost,
For out in the world we find
Success begins with a fellow's WILL —
It's all in the state of the mind.

If you think you're outclassed, you are;
You've got to think high to rise.
You've just got-to-be sure of yourself
Before you can win the prize.

Life's battles don't always go
To the stronger or faster man,
But sooner or later the man who wins
Is the one who THINKS HE CAN.
— AUTHOR UNKNOWN[174]

Successful people who accomplish things have learned to stay
focused on the object at hand or that which is important at that moment. They have trained their minds not to wander or worry about
future events or to be distracted by negative things in the past. Sometimes it is the little pesky thoughts that dominate our thinking.

*It is the little bits of things that fret and worry us; we can dodge an
elephant, but we can't dodge a fly.*
— JOSH BILLINGS

Napoleon had this ability to concentrate on one thing at a time.
He wrote: "The clarity of my ideas and my ability to prolong my occupations indefinitely without experiencing fatigue is explained by
my keeping each object and each business filed in my head as in a
chest of drawers. When I wish to interrupt one occupation, I shut
its drawer and open another. They do not mix, and when I am busy
with one I am not importuned or tired by the other. . . . When I want
to sleep, I shut all the drawers, and I am fast asleep."

Two valuable traits are learning to take first things first and
having the ability to know what they are. President Dwight D.
Eisenhower, thirty-fourth president of the United States, learned
this and stated in his older years, "The older I get, the more wisdom
I find in the ancient rule of taking first things first—a process which
often reduces the most complex human problems to manageable
proportions."

One way of doing this is to write things that need to be done
and then put them in order according to their importance. The great
English statesman, Winston Churchill, found this to be helpful with
all his pressing duties. He said, "It helps to write down half a dozen
things which are worrying me. Two of them, say, disappear; about
two nothing can be done."

People that live a helter-skelter life with nothing written, filed,
or recorded, usually have problems in every area of their lives.

A man's accomplishments in life are the cumulative effect of his attention to detail.
—JOHN FOSTER DULLES (1888-1959)
American lawyer and diplomat who helped formulate the
foreign policies of the United States.

This fact is demonstrated in the life of Andrew Carnegie in the following paragraph, which shows his attention to detail even after he became wealthy and famous:

Carnegie followed costs with an exact, a niggling care. Those who worked under him knew this – and knew that, whether at home or abroad, Carnegie examined the cost sheets for each operation with microscopic attention. Charles Schwab, his chief lieutenant in the late 1890s, described to the Industrial Commission how exact the procedures were: "We made a careful statement of each manufacture, with the cost as compared with each department, and the reasons . . . had the manager of that department make such explanations as were necessary. . . .

"Greater economics are affected by strict supervision over all departments than in any other direction." And another associate, testifying before the Stanley Committee much later, recalled the constant driving presence of the head partner: "A careful record was kept of the costs. You are expected always to get it ten cents cheaper the next year or the next month." And once, among many such occasions, Carnegie, looking at the reports sent to him in Scotland, caught an increase of 5 per cent in coke consumption. He wrote to the manager involved: "This is, at least, 5 per cent more than it should be, and perhaps more. It should be investigated, beginning at the beginning. . . . We should do better than that."[175]

A person is able to keep focused better when he gives attention to details, taking care of things properly as they come but not letting unimportant details keep him from doing the more important things. Carefulness and preparedness pave the way to success:

Success . . . is not often gained by direct effort as by careful, systematic, thorough preparation for duty.
—GEORGE S. BOUTWELL (1818-1905)
In Allen T. Rice, ed., Reminiscences of Abraham Lincoln, 1885

It was the comic entertainer, Eddie Cantor (1892-1964), who made the statement which is so true in many cases: "It took me twenty years to become an overnight success."[176] Benjamin Disraeli said it well: "The secret of success is constancy of purpose."

The ability to know what is the most important matter at hand is the difference between success and failure. To fritter away time on unimportant things is a loss. The question: what is important and what is not? To give attention to details but not be consumed with them is what's important.

> *Don't drown yourself in details. Look at the whole.*
> — FERDINAND POCH (1851-1929)[177]
> In Charles Bugnet, "Power" (The Power to Get Things Done)

This is demonstrated in one of the many incidents that happened in the life of President Lincoln, as stated in the following:

> *Now, my man, go away, go away! I cannot meddle in your case. I could as easily bail out the Potomac River with a teaspoon as attend to all the details of the army.*
> — ABRAHAM LINCOLN (1809-1865)[178]
> Remark to a soldier who in trying to have his grievance with the Army redressed had overstretched Lincoln's patience

Another President found this to be true while involved in leading the nation:

> *"A President who doesn't know how to decentralize, will be weighed down with details, and won't have time to deal with the big issues."*
> — DWIGHT D. EISENHOWER (1890-1969)
> 34th President of the United States (1953-61)

SUCCESS STORY:

SIR WILLIAM OSLER

Osler became the most famous physician of his generation, and organized the world-famous Johns Hopkins School of Medicine. He became Regius Professor of Medicine at Oxford — the highest honor that can be bestowed upon any medical man in the British Empire. He was knighted by the king of England. When he died, two huge volumes containing 1466 pages were required to tell the story of his life.

Dale Carnegie relates in his book, *How to Stop Worrying and*

Start Living, the secret of Sir Osler's success. In 1913, Osler addressed the students of Yale University. He told those Yale students that a man like himself who had been a professor in four universities and had written a popular book was supposed to have "brains of a special quality." He declared that it was untrue. He said that his intimate friends knew that his brains were "of the most mediocre character." The following paragraph is Mr. Carnegie's comments about Dr. Osler:

What, then, was the secret of his success? He stated that it was owing to what he called living in "day-tight compartments." What did he mean by that? A few months before he spoke at Yale, Sir William Osler had crossed the Atlantic on a great ocean liner where the captain, standing on the bridge, could press a button and — presto! — there was a clanging of machinery and various parts of the ship were immediately shut off from one another — shut off into watertight compartments. "Now each one of you," Dr. Osler said to those Yale students, "is a much more marvelous organization that the great liner, and bound on a longer voyage. What I urge is that you so learn to control the machinery as to live with "day-tight compartments" as the most certain way to ensure safety on the voyage. Get on the bridge, and see that at least the great bulkheads are in working order. Touch a button and hear, at every level of your life, the iron doors shutting out the Past — the dead yesterdays. Touch another and shut off, with a metal curtain, the Future — the unborn tomorrows. Then you are safe — safe for today! . . . Shut off the past! Let the dead past bury its dead. . . . Shut out the yesterdays which have lighted fools the way to dusty death. . . . The load of tomorrow, added to that of yesterday, carried today, makes the strongest falter. Shut off the future as tightly as the past. . . . The future is today. . . . The day of man's salvation is now. Waste of energy, mental distress, nervous worries dog the steps of a man who is anxious about the future. . . . Shut close, then, the great fore and aft bulkheads, and prepare to cultivate the habit of "day-tight compartments."[179]

SUCCESS NUGGETS:

Concentrate all your thoughts upon the work at hand. The sun's rays do not burn until brought to a focus.
— ALEXANDER GRAHAM BELL

Concentration is the secret of strength.
— RALPH WALDO EMERSON

No steam or gas drives anything until it is confined. No life ever grows great until it is focused, dedicated, disciplined.
— HARRY EMERSON FOSDICK, DD

Genius is intensity.
— HONORE BALZAC[180]

17
SACRIFICE AND WORK HARD

"Go to the ant, thou sluggard; consider her ways, and be wise
. . . provideth her meat in the summer, and gathereth her food in
the harvest" (Proverbs 6:6, 8).

Sacrifice means to give up something for the sake of something
else. There are many people who want something, but are they willing to sacrifice to get it? This does not mean to sacrifice precious
things such as relationships and family times. It means to give up
idle time for a time of productivity, or extravagant living to realize
a dream.

Several years ago the story was told in *Reader's Digest* about a
young oriental couple who lived in a small room above the bakery
where they both worked. They did not own a car and used a bicy-
cle for transportation. They lived frugally and saved every penny
until they had enough money to buy the bakery when it came up for
sale. They became the new owners simply because of sacrifice, determination, and hard work. They were not asleep in their thoughts
but were on fire with a goal.

Innumerable success stories have been written by people who
have made it. So often their tales are riddled with instances that

show that in the beginning there were sacrifices, hard work, and a relentless pursuit of a dream. While others were living easier lives, they were working hard, pushing triumphantly through impossible situations to victory.

> *The heights by great men reached and kept,*
> *Were not attained by sudden flight;*
> *But they, while their companions slept,*
> *Were toiling upward in the night.*
> — HENRY WADSWORTH LONGFELLOW

Success demands a price. It is the giving of self to the purpose at hand. It costs something to be successful. It does not just happen, but there is giving until there seems to be no more to give.

> *For anything worth having one must pay the price; and the price is always work, patience, love, self-sacrifice — no paper currency, no promises to pay, but the fold of real service.*
> — JOHN BURROUGHS (1837-1921)
> An American naturalist

> *There's no free gate to anything worthwhile: not to skill nor health, nor to success nor friendship, nor even to the lasting love and respect of those who are nearest and dearest to us. These are the items that make up the best income that any human being can have, and the sum of that income will be measured by the sum of what we are willing to pay to get it.*
> — AUTHOR UNKNOWN [181]

Rarely do people become successful by mere accident. Not much of anything good just happens. It usually happens through planning and working the plan. There must be painstaking, careful diligence given to the matter at hand in order to bring it to pass, just as Thomas Edison once said: "I never did anything worth doing by accident nor did any of my inventions come by accident."

"Work," declared Thomas A. Edison, "is measured not by hours, but by what is accomplished." He believed that rewarding toil called for 2 percent inspiration and 98 percent perspiration. He demonstrated this belief by working for days at a time, stopping only for short naps.

Thus, in his effort to make the phonograph reproduce an aspirated sound, he worked from eighteen to twenty hours a day for seven months on the single word "specia." His problem was: "I said into the phonograph, 'specia, specia, specia,' but it responded with 'pecia, pecia, pecia.' It was enough to drive one mad. But I held firm and succeeded."[182]

There will be failures in life, often in the pursuit of a dream, but the key is to not stay in "failure mode" but to keep working at it until success comes.

When I was a young man I observed that nine out of ten things I did were failures. I didn't want to be a failure, so I did ten times more work.
— GEORGE BERNARD SHAW (1856-1950)
British dramatist, playwright, and novelist

Some people don't want to work hard. They would rather sit and do nothing or make excuses why they cannot. They just want to work as little as possible and hope that they make it. They don't want any pain attached to the price tag.

Effort is only effort when it begins to hurt.
— JOSE ORTEGAY GASSET (1883-1955)
Spanish philosopher and writer

The following scriptures states that the diligent shall bear rule and increase; whereas the lazy will have nothing:

Proverbs 13:4: "The soul of the sluggard desireth, and hath nothing: but the soul of the diligent shall be made fat."

Proverbs 12:24: "The hand of the diligent shall bear rule: but the slothful shall be under tribute."

Proverbs 22:13 says that the lazy person always has an excuse: "The slothful man saith, There is a lion without, I shall be slain in the streets." He operates out of fear. His laziness is ruled by a manufactured excuse. As also in Proverbs 20:4: "The sluggard will not plow by reason of the cold; therefore shall he beg in harvest and have nothing." I say, "Put on a coat and get to work!"

Those who are diligent are hard working and give careful attention to details. The opposite is lazy and careless. Proverbs 18:9 gives example of this: "He also that is slothful in his work is brother to him that is a great waster." The question is, "Who do you allow your brother to be?" — A waster or a hard worker.

Often those who make it are the ones who work harder and longer than others, and keep going even when it's tough and failure seems imminent.

Investigation into the lives of the great men of our age and past ages, will show that these men of mark and grand performance outstayed other men, worked harder than other men, worked longer than other men, and had great strength and stamina.
— WILLIAM BLAIKIE (1820-1899)
American lawyer, athlete, and promoter of physical training
Published *How to Get Strong and How to Stay So*

People who mismanage their time and take the easier route in life are often the ones who have the most excuses and cry the loudest of how life has treated them. Some lament about the bad luck or the bad home life they have experienced, but there are many who had the same bad luck but refused to succumb to what was handed to them. Then there are those who tell others about their bad luck, who have had great opportunities but neglected to take advantage of them.

It will generally be found that men who are constantly lamenting their ill luck are only reaping the consequences of their own neglect, mismanagement, and improvidence, or want of application.
— SAMUEL SMILES (1812-1904)
Scottish biographical author

Life is not easy and there are situations that are hard, but we can grieve about it or we can begin to work at removing or changing the negative circumstance until it becomes a positive one. Is it easy? No, a thousand times no! But it can be overcome with hard work and determination. It is bit by bit, a little here, a little there. Eventually the job is done and the dream is realized. The mountain can be moved!

The man who removes a mountain begins by carrying away small stones.
— CHINESE PROVERB

To succeed requires hard work. Not many things just happen by themselves. Think of the bridges built, the churches erected, or businesses realized. They are the results of plans and work to accomplish them.

Remember that the faith that removes mountains always carries a pick.
— ANONYMOUS

So start working at it stone by stone, chip by chip. It doesn't matter how hard or big the job. It matters that you put your heart into it and give it your best shot. Life should be lived in such a way that there is pleasure in working. It should not be a drudge or something dreadful, but time enjoyed.

The following men, who are remembered for their contribution to the betterment of mankind, were not idle, did not pause too long, but worked hard toward their goals until they were completed even though it took some of them half a lifetime to accomplish:

- *Noah Webster* labored thirty-six years writing his dictionary, crossing the Atlantic twice to gather material.

- *John Milton* rose at 4:00 AM every day in order to have enough hours for his *Paradise Lost.*

- *Edward Gibbon* spent twenty-six years on his *Decline and Fall of the Roman Empire.*

- *George Stephenson* spent fifteen years to perfect the locomotive.

- *James Watt*, a Scottish engineer, worked for thirty years on the condensing engine.

- *Cyrus W. Field* crossed the ocean fifty times to lay a cable so men could talk across the oceans. The first fully successful cable was laid in 1866, after four previous attempts. Field promoted the first cable to be laid across the Atlantic in 1857. It broke 360 miles from shore. A second attempt in June 1858 also failed. In 1865, Field chartered the steamship *Great Eastern* to lay a new cable. The cable broke when the project was almost done.

- *George Westinghouse*, an American inventor, was treated as a mild lunatic by most railroad executives. "Stopping a train by the wind! The man's crazy," was often said about him. Yet he persevered and finally sold the air-brake idea.

- *Sir Walter Scott* put in fifteen hours a day at his desk, rising at four o'clock in the morning. He averaged a book every two months and turned out the "Waverly Novels" at one a month (and that was without computers).

Sacrifice and Work Hard

- *Virgil* spent seven years on his *Georgics* and twelve on the *Aeneid.*

- *William Cullen Bryant* (1794-1878), editor, critic, biographer, naturalist, and civic leader, is best remembered as the Father of American Poetry. He rewrote one of his poetic masterpieces ninety-nine times before publication, and it became a classic.

- *Adam Clark* spent forty years writing his *Commentary* on the Holy Scriptures.

- *George Bancroft* used twenty-six years of his life on *History of the United States.*

- *Ernest Hemingway* (1899-1961) is said to have gone over the manuscript of *The Old Man and the Sea* eighty times.

This is the day to move forward, even if inch by inch. To sit still too long is to rust. To pause beyond the pause is to stagnate, just as unmoving water stagnates.

> *Even if you're on the right track, you'll get run over if you just sit there.*
>
> —WILL ROGERS (1879-1935)
> American writer, humorist, and actor

SUCCESS STORY:

ENRICO CARUSO

Enrico Caruso shared how his success was not easy but was work:

"When people think I sing freely and think I take the life easy on the stage, they mistake. At such time I am working at the top of my strength. I must not show that I work when I sing—that is what is art."[183]

In 1945, Dorothy Caruso, the wife of Enrico, who became the greatest singer in the world in his day, wrote the book *Enrico Caruso, His Life and Death.* She shares the following story, which demonstrates the sacrifice he made to become a great singer:

> *One afternoon when the household was busy with preparations for the journey he came into the salon, sat down beside me and announced, "I have a new servant, I am taking him with me to Mexico."*

186

"Who is he? Do you know him?" I asked anxiously.

"Yes," he said slowly, *"yes, I know him. He came to ask for work this morning. I told him if he wished to be the valet of my valet he could stay. I will tell you a story. When I was young, doing my military duty in Naples, I wanted to sing. My sergeant helped me to have an audition with Maestro Vergine. He was a great teacher. He heard me sing and said, 'You have a voice like the wind in the shutters.' I felt very bad, but he had a class of pupils, and I asked if I could listen while he taught them. He said yes. He had a daughter who was engaged to his best pupil, a man named Punzo. This Punzo was a proud and stupid man, but the Maestro said that one day he would be the greatest tenor in the world. I spent my free time listening to the lessons. I sat in a corner and no one noticed me. Then my brother took my military duty for me – very kind of him – and I spent more time in the class. My black suit had turned green, so I bought a little bottle of dye and dyed it and pressed it before I went. My stepmother cut my shirt fronts from paper, so I would look nice. I had to walk very far every day to get there – shoes cost money, so I sang at weddings and funerals to make a little. I remember the first pair of shoes I bought myself – very pretty, but the soles were cardboard. Halfway to the Maestro's house came the rain. My beautiful shoes were wet. I took them off and put them by the stove to dry. They curled up and I walked home on bare feet. At the end of the year the pupils had their examination. When all had finished I asked the Maestro if I could try too. 'What! You still here?' he said, but he let me sing. 'You have no voice,' he said, 'but you have the intelligence – you have learned something.' He got me my first little engagement. He was very kind to me when I was young and poor. Punzo married the girl but did not become anything. He is the man who came this morning – and he is still very proud and stupid."*

"But why do you want him then?"

"Because I will show him how to be a good valet – then he will know something and not be stupid any more."[184]

Not only did Caruso have a *big* voice, but he also had a *big* heart, which the following incident illustrates: At the end of Enrico's life, he told his wife, "Poor Punzo, I tell you something, Doro, only he does not know. I bought for him a nice house in Naples and put money in the bank for him and his wife. He will have big surprise.

Sacrifice and Work Hard

We will tell no one in Naples that he was my servant — we say he is my assistant. Punzo is a proud man, and here is his home."[185]

> *The requisites of a singer — a big chest, a big mouth, 90 per cent memory, 10 per cent intelligence, lots of hard work, and something in the heart.*[186]
>
> — ENRICO CARUSO

SUCCESS NUGGETS:

> *"Seeds of success won't work, if you won't!"*

> *There is but one easy place in this world, and that is the grave.*
>
> — BEECHER[187]

> *I believe that one's success depends not upon his location, but upon his Industry, Integrity, and Vision; not upon his friends, but upon what he thoroughly learns to do himself; not upon luck, but upon Work, stick-to-itiveness and pluck — whole-heartedly and enthusiastically minding and watching his step.*
>
> — E. L. KIRKPATRICK[188]

> *A truly great man, is one whose body has been trained to be the servant of his mind; whose passions are trained to be the servants of his will; who enjoys the beautiful, loves truth, hates wrong, loves to do good, and respects others as himself.*[189]

> *Whatever you have received more than others in health, in talents, in ability, in success, in a pleasant childhood, in harmonious conditions of home life, all this you must not take to yourself as a matter of course. You must pay a price for it. You must render an unusually great sacrifice of your life for other life.*
>
> — ALBERT SCHWEITZER[190]

> *If at first you don't succeed, try, try again.*
>
> — T. H. PALMER (in *Teacher's Manual*, 1840, p. 223)

18
DEVELOP
WILLPOWER

"Choose ye this day whom ye will serve" (Joshua 24:15).

Everyone will choose to develop willpower and make right choices, or he or she will just be like a leaf floating down the river, allowing itself be guided by the tide and currents of the water. Everyone will serve something! So choose well, for choices determine your destiny!

Will is a disposition, choice, determination, insistence, persistence, or willfulness. It is the mental power manifested as choosing, desiring, or acting according to principles. Look out for the person who makes up his mind that he is going to do something. He usually does. Philip Sidney, who gave his life for his country, is famous for saying the following:

> *Either I will find a way, or I will make one.*
> —PHILIP SIDNEY (1554-1586)
> Courtier, traveler, poet, patron, and soldier during reign of Queen Elizabeth I. He gave his life for his country.

Mary Roberts Rinehart, author of more than fifty novels, tells how she became an author. She made a way even when there seemed to be no way, as the following story demonstrates:

"I always thought I could learn to write, if I just had the time, but I had three small sons, and my husband to look after . . . also, my mother, who for several years was a helpless invalid. Then, during a financial panic, we lost everything. I was driven frantic by debts. I made up my mind I was going to earn some money by writing, so I made up a schedule, planning every hour for the week in advance. Certain periods during the day and in the evening after I got the children off to bed while Dr. Rinehart was out making calls, I set aside for writing."[191]

Mary Rinehart had the will, but she needed a plan to execute the will, as the following poem depicts:

A WILL DEMANDS A PLAN

There may be nothing wrong with you,
The way you live, the work you do,
But I can very plainly see
Exactly what is wrong with me.
It isn't that I'm indolent
Or dodging duty by intent;
I work as hard as anyone,
And yet I get so little done,
The morning goes, the noon is here,
Before I know, the night is near,
And all around me, I regret,
Are things I haven't finished yet.
If I could just get organized!
I oftentimes have realized
Not all that matters is the *man*;
The man must also have a plan.

With you, there may be nothing wrong,
But here's my trouble right along;
I do the things that don't amount
To very much, of no account,
That really seems important though
And let a lot of matters go.
I nibble this, I nibble that,

But never finish what I'm at.
I work as hard as anyone,
And yet, I get so little done,
I'd do so much you'd surprised,
If I could just get organized! [192]

The key is to get organized in your mind. Know what you want, plan to make it happen, and take it a day at a time, step by step, minute by minute. Most great things do not happen overnight or in a short time. Sometimes the process seems like it takes forever. Instead of throwing in the towel and becoming more frustrated because you cannot seem to make something happen, examine your efforts. Ask yourself, "What are my plans to reach my goals?"

After plans are made, then it is time to execute the will. A will is recognized and respected by all manner of people from kings to peasants. Even death respects a person's will, as demonstrated in the following poem:

WILL

There is no chance, no destiny, no fate,
Can circumvent or hinder or control
The firm resolve of a determined soul.
Gifts count for nothing; will alone is great;
All things give way before it, soon or late.
What obstacle can stay the mighty force
Of the sea-seeking river in its course,
Or cause the ascending orb of day to wait?
Each wellborn soul must win what it deserves:
Let the fool prate of luck. The fortunate
Is he whose earnest purpose never swerves,
Whose slightest action or inaction serves
The one great aim. Why, even Death stands still,
And waits an hour sometimes for such a will.

— ELLA WHEELER WILCOX (1830-1893) [193]
American journalist and poet

Many people have strength and desire, but they lack will. The world is full of people who are someday going to do this or do that, but somehow they never get around to doing it. A will can motivate a person to be determined to finish what he intends or makes up his mind to do.

Develop Willpower

> *People do not lack strength; they lack will.*
> — VICTOR HUGO (1802-1885)

Hugo was a French poet, dramatist, novelist, essayist, and critic. "He was a many-sided genius, whose work is outstanding in quantity, quality and variety. Hugo worked hard through-out most of his long life. He was alert to all the political, social, artistic and literary events of his day, and most of them are reflected in his writings." He had written twenty-three poems when he was only fourteen. Before he was twenty-one, his work won praise from Francois de Chateaubriand, one of the leading writers of that time.

One of Hugo's most famous plays, *Les Miserables* (1862), deals with an ex-convict, Jean Valjean, and his attempts to lead an upright life in Paris during the 1800s. Many critics also regard him as France's greatest poet.

Hugo felt that a poet had a duty as a leader, and this thrust him into politics. At first Hugo supported Napoleon for president, but when Napoleon made himself emperor and abolished the constitution, Hugo helped lead the opposition against Napoleon. He wrote the pamphlet entitled *Napoleon the Insignificant* and other writings against him. He was later forced to flee to Brussels and ended up on Guernsey Island, where he lived and wrote while in exile, until the Germans defeated France at the battle of Sidon in 1870. Hugo returned to Paris to aid his countrymen and to endure the siege of the city. He always remained steadfast in his opposition of tyranny, and he is remembered for his devotion to such humanitarian causes as free compulsory education and universal suffrage.

Often people are thought to be part genius or smarter than others who accomplish things that other people wish they could do. The truth is that in most cases it is not genius; it is a made-up mind or a strong will that will not stop until they get the results they are working toward.

Genius is only the power of making continuous efforts. The line between failure and success is so fine that we scarcely know when we pass it: so fine that we are often on the line and do not know it. How many a man has thrown up his hands at a time when a little more effort, a little more patience, would have achieved success. As the tide goes clear out, so it comes clear in. In business, sometimes, prospects may seem darkest when really they are on the turn. A little more persistence, a little more effort, and what seemed hopeless failure may

turn to glorious success. There is no failure except in no longer try-
ing. There is no defeat except from within, no really insurmountable
barrier save our own inherent weakness of purpose.
— ELBERT HUBBARD (1856-1915)[194]

Inherent weakness of purpose or will has caused many to fail
or to give up. They do not want something bad enough to endure
the pain of achieving. Success is achieved by continuous effort and
painstaking effort even when it is fraught with difficulties.

SUCCESS
If you want a thing bad enough
To go out and fight for it,
Work day and night for it,
Give up your time and your peace and your sleep for it,
If only desire of it
Makes you quite mad enough
Never to tire of it,
Makes you hold all other things tawdry and cheap for it,
If life seems all empty and useless without it
And all that you scheme and you dream is about it,
If gladly you'll sweat for it,
Fret for it,
Plan for it,
If you'll simply go after that thing that you want,
With all your capacity,
Strength and sagacity,
Faith, hope and confidence, stern pertinacity,
If neither cold poverty, famished and gaunt,
Nor sickness nor pain
Of body and brain
Can turn you away from the thing that you want,
If dogged and grim you besiege and beset it,
    You'll get it.
— BERTON BRALEY [195]

The Chinese proverb says, "Great souls have wills; feeble ones
have only wishes." The difference between a will and a wish is the
ability to work at something and make it happen even if it takes a
long time. Time is not the main thing. The main thing is the keeping
on until it is done.

Develop Willpower

> *The secret to success is constancy to purpose.*
> — BENJAMIN DISRAELI

Constancy, persistency, and an attitude of not giving up no matter, is what it takes to win. There has to be that magical feeling inside, that will, a bulldog tenacity that says, "I'm going to win!" It does not matter the obstacles, the frustrations, the setbacks, the hard work, or long hours of disappointments, what matters is that you know deep within that you are going to win!

> *It is fatal to enter any war without the will to win it.*
> — DOUGLAS MACARTHUR (1880-1964)
> One of the leading American generals of World War II

I say it is fatal to enter life without the will to win!

SUCCESS STORY:

DOUGLAS MACARTHUR

MacArthur gallantly defended Bataan Peninsula in the Philippine Islands in the early days of World War II and later led the Allied forces to victory in the Southwest Pacific. Late in 1942, he opened a three-year offensive against the Japanese. By early 1944, his troops had freed most of New Guinea, New Britain, the Solomons, and the Admiralty Islands.

MacArthur held the rank of colonel when the United States entered World War I in 1917. He won fame as a front-line general during the war in France in the battles of the Meuse-Argonne and Saint-Mihiel. He was wounded three times, decorated thirteen times, and cited for bravery in action seven times. In 1930, he became a four-star general and was named Army Chief of Staff, the youngest in US history.

MacArthur became a five-star general of the army in December 1944. He took command of all American army forces in the Pacific in April 1945. During this period, MacArthur showed great military genius and personal bravery. President Truman announced the Japanese acceptance of Allied surrender terms on August 14, 1965. Truman made MacArthur supreme commander for the Allied Powers.

As supreme commander, it was MacArthur's job to receive the surrender and to rule Japan. He accepted the Japanese surrender aboard the battleship *Missouri* on September 2, 1945.

He set up headquarters in Tokyo and became the sole administrator of the military government in Japan. His firm but fair methods soon won him the respect of the Japanese, who had feared a harsh occupation.

On April 18, 1951, MacArthur flew to San Francisco. It was his first return to his homeland since 1935. Next morning he was given an official welcome at the city hall. It had been arranged that he should make a speech to Congress, and at San Francisco a message arrived that the text must be submitted to the Department of the Army. He protested, and the department canceled the instruction and apologized. When he arrived in Washington, after midnight, a crowd of some twenty thousand welcomed him. Marshall and the Joint Chiefs were in the official party.

Next day, the 19th, the cars of MacArthur and his party, driving to the Congress building, passed more cheering crowds. On arrival he was led to the Chamber of the House of Representatives, where he spoke from the rostrum to the members of both houses. The speech, some 3,500 words long, was MacArthur at his best — stately, modest, ornamented as always with flashes of rhetoric. He spoke as a fellow American. In general he repeated the arguments he had been using during the last year and more, and wound up:

> *I am closing my fifty-two years of military service. When I joined the Army, even before the turn of the century, it was the fulfillment of all my boyish hopes and dreams. The world has turned over many times since I took the oath on the Plain at West Point, and the hopes and dreams have long vanished. But I still remember the refrain of one of the most popular barrack ballads of that day, which proclaimed, most proudly, that "Old soldiers never, never die. They just fade away."*
>
> *And like the old soldier of that ballad, I now close my military career and just fade away — an old soldier who tried to do his duty as God gave him the light to see that duty.*
>
> *Goodbye.*[196]

MacArthur died on April 5, 1964, at the age of eighty-four. President Lyndon B. Johnson called him "one of America's greatest heroes" and proclaimed a week of public mourning.

During World War II, on February 8, 1942, President Quezon of the Philippines sent a message to President Roosevelt proposing that the United States immediately grant the Philippines independence, that the islands be neutralized, the American and Japanese forces withdrawn, and the Philippine Army disband. MacArthur added a long dispatch, warning Marshall that his forces were "near done" and their "complete destruction" might come at any time. "So far as the military angle is concerned," he added, "the problem presents itself as to whether the plan of President Quezon might offer the best possible solution of what is about to be a disastrous *debacle.*"

This shocked Roosevelt, who wrote in his diary that Quezon's message was "wholly unreal" and took no account of "what the war was for or what the well known characteristics of Japan towards conquered people were." President Roosevelt authorized MacArthur to arrange for a capitulation of the Filipino elements of his forces if necessary, but added:

American forces will continue to keep our flag flying in the Philippines so long as there remains any possibility of resistance. I have made these decisions in complete understanding of your military estimate that accompanied President Quezon's message to me. The duty and the necessity of resisting Japanese aggression to the last transcend in importance any other obligation now facing us in the Philippines.

There has been gradually welded into a common front a globe-encircling opposition to the predatory powers that are seeing the destruction of individual liberty and freedom of government. We cannot afford to have this line broken in any particular theatre. As the most powerful member of this coalition we cannot display weakness in fact or in spirit anywhere. It is mandatory that there be established once and for all in the minds of all peoples complete evidence that the American determination and indomitable will to win carries on down to the last unit.[197]

President Roosevelt described this was what helped win World War II: *The determination and indomitable will to win.*

SUCCESS NUGGETS:

Faith bestows that sublime courage that rises superior to the troubles and disappointments of life, that acknowledges no defeat except as a step to victory; that is strong to endure, patient to wait, and energetic to struggle. . . . Light up, then, the lamp of faith in your heart. . . . It will lead you safely through the mists of doubt and the black darkness of de-

spair; along the narrow, thorny ways of sickness and sorrow, and over
the treacherous places of temptation and uncertainty.
— JAMES ALLEN[198]

*Nothing can withstand the power of the human will if it is willing to
stake its very existence to the extent of its purpose.*
— BENJAMIN DISRAELI

*We are not sent into this world to do anything into which we cannot
put our hearts. We have certain work to do for our bread and that is to be
done strenuously, other work to do for our delight and that is to be done
heartily; neither is to be done by halves of shifts, but with a will; and what
is not worth this effort is not to be done at all.*[199]
— JOHN RUSKIN (1819-1900)
English poet and author

19
TREAT PEOPLE RIGHT

"And as ye would that men should do to you, do ye also to them likewise" (Luke 6:31).

Respect and consideration for others is mandatory for true success. Courtesy is a general allowance for someone despite the way the other person acts. Your behavior should not be determined by other people's actions but by a set of predetermined attitudes. Consideration, cooperation, and generosity are the prerequisites for a success-filled life.

True success is measured not by how high people climb but by how many people they have helped and how kind they were to others on their way there. A former Chinese minister to the United States, Mr. Wu-Tung-Fang, once said of Abraham Lincoln: "His benevolence was boundless, his wisdom was profound; to anyone approaching him he had the genial warmth of the sun."[200]

Push as hard as you may at the gate of success, it will creak and stick unless you oil its hinges with courtesy.
— AUTHOR UNKNOWN

Mother Teresa not only was courteous to other people, she went beyond the courtesy level to the level of love. There are many stories about her love, but the following one depicts her level of love:

It is said that when she went to Calcutta, on her very first day, she saw a man lying in the gutter covered with disease and filth, and no one would go near him. She kneeled down next to him, held his frail body in her arms, and began cleaning him. He was so astonished he asked her, "Why are you doing this?" Her simple reply was, "Because I love you."

She was known to have said the following: "Spread love everywhere you go: first of all in your own house. Give love to your children, to your wife or husband, to a next door neighbor. . . Let no one ever come to you without leaving better and happier. Be the living expression of God's kindness; kindness in your face, kindness in your eyes, kindness in your smile, kindness in your warm greeting."

Treating others right is not only important for the receiver, but just as important for the giver. It brings health, joy, and happiness, as the following quotes depict:

> *Doing good to others is not a duty. It is a joy, for it increases your own health and happiness.*
> — ZOROASTER (about 1000 BC)
> Philosopher

> *Proverbs 15:24: "Pleasant words are as an honeycomb, sweet to the soul, and health to the bones."*

How you treat others will come back to you, so seek to be kind, loving, and considerate. Be good to yourself by being good to those with whom you come in contact.

> *When you are good to others, you are best to yourself.*
> — BENJAMIN FRANKLIN (1706-1790) [201]
> American statesman, author, inventor, printer, and scientist

Not only are you good to yourself by being kind, but it is a healthy practice as well. It breeds good feelings within. There is a glow that spreads to every organ of the body and a sense of goodwill that penetrates the heart and emotions.

> *Love cures people — both the ones who give it and the ones who receive it.*
> — DR. KARL MENNINGER
> Psychiatrist and co-founder of The Menninger Clinic and Foundation in Topeka, Kansas

Life is difficult enough just coping with everyday living, so why not try to turn it into a garden of kindness? No one lives to himself. We are all connected and need to help one another and to try to bring a smile to the faces of those about us. There are so many lonely hearts, and hiding behind the public masks that people put on, there is many times a need for kindness and understanding. Think kindness and bring gladness to others, and you will be happier!

Life is short and we have never too much time for gladdening the hearts of those who are traveling the dark journey with us. Oh, be swift to love, make haste to be kind!
— HENRY AMIEL (1821-1881)

Great people are kind. If there is someone who appears to be successful but who is rude and offensive to others, he has empty success. He is not truly great.

The greater man – the greater courtesy.
— ALFRED LORD TENNYSON (1809-1892)[202]

Greatness is demonstrated not in money, possessions, titles, or fame, but the true inner core of a person is revealed in how he or she interacts with people, the known and the unknown. Manners should not be reserved for royalty and the famous, but the smallest child or the least person should be treated with kindness and courtesy. This is the mark of greatness.

"'Glad rags' do not indicate superiority. All some people have they put into showy finery. Real greatness consists in beautiful garments clothing the mind and sweet kindnesses adorning the human spirit. Finery never covers up the nakedness of the mind and character."[203]

A great man shows his greatness by the way he treats little men.
— THOMAS CARLYLE (1795-1881)
Scottish-born English prose writer. He is remembered for his explosive attacks on sham, hypocrisy, and excessive materialism.

Great people do not speak ill of others. They always try to lift others and encourage them to be successful. Mark the person who is known as a gossip and challenge yourself to not be known as one. Instead make it a priority to not drag people down but to encourage and say things that will lift them up! As you lift them, you are lifting yourself; you are not allowing yourself to dwell in the gutter of malicious gossip.

> *No man can hold another man in the gutter without remaining there himself.*
> — BOOKER T. WASHINGTON

The character trait of truly great people is that they do not gossip or tear down other people. Enrico Caruso, the world's greatest singer in his day, observed the following: "Why do they talk and waste their time?" he said one night after a dinner party. "If there is something good to say, speak—otherwise be quiet."[204]

Before you criticize someone, think twice. Even if they deserve it, there are ways to say things to get the point across without offending someone.

> *When dealing with people, let us remember we are not dealing with creatures of logic. We are dealing with creatures of emotion, creatures bristling with prejudices and motivated by pride and vanity. . . . And criticism is a dangerous spark—a spark that is liable to cause an explosion in the power magazine of pride—an explosion that sometimes hastens death.*
> — DALE CARNEGIE (1888-1955)
> An American pioneer in public speaking and personality development

Proverbs 15:1 states: "A soft answer turneth away wrath: but grievous words stir up anger."

Personal contention and bristling emotions are the cause of more trouble than can be mentioned. It is best to learn how to get along instead of flaring up in anger.

> *No man who is resolved to make the most of himself, can spare time for personal contention. Still less can he afford to take the consequences, including the vitiation of his temper and the loss of self-control. Yield larger things to which you show no more than equal rights; and yield lesser ones though clearly your own. Better give your path to a dog than be bitten by him in contesting for the right. Even killing the dog would not cure the bite.*
> — ABRAHAM LINCOLN
> Spoken to a young army officer for indulging in a violent controversy with an associate

Remember that charity thinketh no evil, much less repeats it. There are two good rules which ought to be written on every heart; never believe anything bad about anybody unless you positively know it is true; never tell even that unless you feel that it is absolutely necessary and that God is listening while you tell it.
— VAN DYKE[205]

Everyone works better when he or she is appreciated. This is the opinion of many successful people, among them Charles Schwab. Andrew Carnegie paid Charles Schwab a million dollars a year because of his ability to deal with people. When asked what his secret was, Schwab gave the following answer:

I consider my ability to arouse enthusiasm among the men, the greatest asset I possess, and the way to develop the best that is in a man is by appreciation and encouragement.

There is nothing else that so kills the ambitions of a man as criticisms from his superiors. I never criticize anyone. I believe in giving a man incentive to work. So I am anxious to praise but loath to find fault. If I like anything I am hearty in my approbation and lavish in my praise.

I have yet to find the man, however great or exalted his station, who did not do better work and put forth greater effort under a spirit of approval than he would ever do under a spirit of criticism.[206]

Remember that other people have good ideas also. Listen to them. Learn to work together and not be so pompous that you have room only for yourself and your ideas.

It is the individual who is not interested in his fellow men who has the greatest difficulties in life and provides the greatest injury to others. It is from among such individuals that all human failures spring.
— ALFRED ADLER (1870-1937)
Austrian psychologist and author

One of the great inventors in America, the man who produced the first Model T automobile, learned to work with others and to respect their ideas and opinions. We would do well to learn from his following advice:

If there is any one secret of success, it lies in the ability to get the other person's point of view and see things from his angle as well as from your own.
— HENRY FORD

SUCCESS STORY:

BENJAMIN FRANKLIN

If you argue and rankle and contradict, you may achieve a victory sometimes; but it will be an empty victory because you will never get your opponent's good will.
— BENJAMIN FRANKLIN (1706-1790)
American statesman, author, inventor, printer, and Scientist

The above words were spoken by a man who as a blundering youth received the following rebuke from an old Quaker friend:

"Ben, you are impossible. Your opinions have a slap in them for everyone who differs with you. They have become so offensive that nobody cares for them. Your friends find they enjoy themselves better when you are not around. You know so much that no man can tell you anything."

After Benjamin Franklin was reprimanded by his friend, he changed his rude, opinionated ways. He said, "I made it a rule to forbear all direct contradiction to the sentiment of others, and all positive assertion of my own. I even forbade myself the use of every word or expression in the language that imported a fix'd opinion, such as 'certainly,' 'undoubtedly,' etc., and I adopted, instead of them, 'I conceive,' I apprehend,' or 'I imagine' a thing to be so or so, or 'it so appears to me at present.' When another asserted something that I thought an error, I deny'd myself the pleasure of contradicting him abruptly, and of showing immediately some absurdity in his proposition: and in answering I began by observing that in certain cases or circumstances his opinion would be right. I soon found the advantage of this change in my manner; the conversations I engag'd in went on more pleasantly. The modest way in which I propos'd my opinions procur'd them a readier reception and less contradiction; I had less mortification when I was found to be in the wrong, and I more easily prevail'd with others to give up their mistakes and join with me when I happened to be in the right."

SUCCESS NUGGETS:

Love is always building up. It puts some line of beauty on every life it touches. It gives new hope to discouraged ones, new strength to those who are weak, new joys to those who are sorrowing. It helps the despairing to rise and start again. It makes life seem more worthwhile to everyone into whose eyes it looks. Its words are benedictions. Its very breath is full of inspiration.
— THE WESTMINISTER TEACHER[207]

Pass smoothly over the perverseness of those you have to do with, and go straight forward. It is abundantly sufficient that you have the testimony of a good conscience toward God.
— JOHN WESLEY[208]

Be good, get good, and do good. Do all the good you can; to all the people you can; in all the ways you can; as often as you can; and as long as you can.
— SPURGEON[209]

The habit of judging and condemning others is usually a great deal more serious blemish than are the things we so glibly point out as flaws or faults.[210]

Life is like a keyboard. The Master's fingers will sweep over it, and a weary world will catch notes of melody as we go along. The life that is in tune with God is keyed to the note of love.
— J. R. MILLER[211]

"A man that hath friends must shew himself friendly."
— PROVERBS 18:24

20
NEVER GIVE UP!

"Therefore, my beloved brethren, be ye stedfast, unmoveable, always abounding in the work of the Lord, forasmuch as ye know that your labour is not in vain in the Lord" (I Corinthians 15:58).

It is God's will for every person to be steadfast, never giving up, and abounding in that which the Lord has called him or her to do. All labor will have its reward. It is imperative no matter what happens to not give up! The story is told of how Winston Churchill addressed a college graduation with just three words. He walked with his cane to the podium and said loudly, "Never give up!" He stepped back three paces, raised his cane slightly, and said once more in a bolder tone, "Never give up!" He then raised his cane straight up, lifted his voice, and thundered, "Never give up!"

Stunned, the audience watched him turn, then go and be seated. When the impact of the address had sunk in, the college students burst into applause, stood to their feet and cheered wildly.

Never give up! If adversity presses,
Providence wisely has mingled the cup,
And the best counsel, in all your distresses,

Never Give Up

Is the stout watchword of "Never give up."
— MARTIN F. TUPPER (1810-1889)[212]
English poet

The gift of being able to never give up and to keep on, even when things look impossible is a great gift to have. All people have been given a will, but some develop the will to greater perfection than others simply by sheer determination. This continual work and spirit of determination eventually cause the traits to become part of the person. Perseverance is going on even when one would like to quit.

Great works are performed, not by strength, but perseverance.
— SAMUEL JOHNSON (1727-1819)
A conservative American political and educational leader, one of the signers of the United States Constitution

In the stormy North Sea off the coast of the Netherlands lay a ledge of rocks where many vessels had been wrecked. Pirates who looted vessels inhabited the island and murdered crews. Finally the Netherlands government determined to rid the island of pirates and assigned Edward Bok's father, a young Dutch lawyer, to do the job.

It was a grim place, barren of trees or any living green thing, but the young lawyer cleaned up the island and not only decided to make it his home but determined to make the island beautiful. He led seafaring men to inhabit the island and said to them. "We must have trees." They were too busy with their fishing and he was compelled to say, "I'll have the trees if I must plant them myself."

"Your trees will never live," said the islanders. "The north winds and storms will kill them all." But plant trees he did, a hundred the first year. The second year he planted more, and each year for the fifty years he lived on the island, he planted trees.

As the trees grew tall through the years, the island became a bird sanctuary. In time, bird lovers from all parts of the world came to this island to study the thousands of birds that rested here.

Then one night something interesting happened. A pair of storm-driven nightingales found refuge in the island. In gratitude for their refuge they remained on the island and raised their young nightingales. Within a few years the island became a colony for nightingales. Throughout Holland and Europe, the fame of the Island of Nightingales spread.

American artist, William M. Chase, took his pupils there each year. "In all the world today," he asserted, "there is no more beautiful place."[213]

Just holding on, not letting go, grasping to a dream, working hard to make it happen even when there seems to be no hope often mark when the turning point comes.

When you get in a tight place and everything goes against you, till it seems as though you could not hold on a minute longer, never give up then, for that is just the place and time that the tide will turn.[ccxiv]
— HARRIETT BEECHER STOWE (1811-1896)
American writer

The wonderful thing about achieving is the day when it finally happens. To hang on, to pursue the prize even when it is out of reach, and then to attain it is an exhilarating experience, as the following poem depicts:

THE GRANDEST PRIZE

In summing up the things to praise,
For what they do for me,
There's one to which I give first place,
Whose virtues plain I see.
I pay it well-earned tribute,
For it to me doth teach
Life's greatest, noblest lesson,
'Tis the prize beyond my reach.

It dares me come and take it,
It says to me, "You know
By struggle and by effort
Your strength and skill will grow;
I'll not surrender tamely,
Tho' you wheedle and beseech,
But if you toil you'll win me,
Tho' now beyond your reach."

And I have found that always
Whene'er I use my skill,
My muscle and intelligence,

My energy and will,
I'm always sure to win it,
And sweet beyond all speech
Is the rapture of the capture
Of the prize once out of reach.
          —WILLIAM T. CARD [215]
          American poet

Just keep reaching, keep going forward even when you are surrounded by obstacles. Never back up when faced with disappointments, but keep attacking your enemies and fears. To win is to dare and to venture forth no matter what is in the way of your dreams.

Rremember this maxim: Attacking is the only secret. Dare and the world always yields; or if it beats you sometimes, dare it again and it will succumb.
          —WILLIAM M. THACKERAY (1811-1863)
          English writer

The thirtieth president of the United States knew this to be true. In spite of the personal challenges and difficulties that he faced during his administration, he summed his philosophy up in the following words:

Nothing in this world can take the place of persistence. Talent will not; nothing is more common than unsuccessful people with talent. Genius will not; unrewarded genius is almost a proverb. Education will not; the world is full of educated derelicts.
          —CALVIN COOLIDGE (1872-1922)

This is true in the case of John Barrymore. A newspaperman called backstage one night to interview John Barrymore after his fifty-sixth performance of Hamlet. The reporter had to wait an hour and a half until after rehearsal. When the great actor finally appeared, the reporter said, "Mr. Barrymore, I'm surprised that you would need a rehearsal after fifty-six performances on Broadway. Why, you're being acclaimed the greatest Hamlet of all time and a genius of the stage!"

Barrymore bent over laughing. "Listen, he said, "Do you want to know the truth? For five months, nine hours every day, I read, re-read, studied, and recited that part. I thought I'd never get it into my head. Several times I wanted to quit. I thought I'd missed my calling, and that it was a mistake for me ever to have gone into acting. Yes, a year ago, I wanted to *quit,* and now they are calling me a genius. Isn't that ridiculous?"[216]

No matter where you have been, what life has handed you, or if you have failed, today is a new day! There are always new opportunities. Failures must be put behind you, and you must step forward into your future. This is your year to be up and going again toward your goals, as the following poem depicts:

THIS YEAR IS YOURS

God built and launched this year for you;
Upon the bridge you stand;
It's your ship, aye, your own ship
And you are in command.
Just what the twelve months' trip will do
Rests wholly, solely, friend with you!

Your log book, kept from day to day,
My friend what will it show?
Have you on your appointed way
Made progress . . . yes or no?
The log will tell, like guiding star,
The sort of Captain that you are.

Contrary winds may oft beset,
Mountainous seas may press,
Fierce storms prevail and false light lure,
You even may know real stress.
Yet, does God's hand hold fast the helm,
There's naught can e'er your ship o'erwhelm.

For weal or woe, this year is yours;
For ship is on life's sea;
Your acts, as captain, must decide
Whichever it shall be;
So now, in starting on your trip,
Ask God to help you sail your ship.

Flower in the crannied wall,
I pluck you out of the crannies,

> I hold you here, root and all, in my hand,
> Little flower—but if I could understand
> What you are, root and all, and all in all,
> I should know what God and man is.
> —ALFRED LORD TENNYSON[217]

Encourage yourself in spite of whatever happens. Pray for strength to do, and strength to become, and you will be strong. The strong ones are those who overcome and win.

BE STRONG

Be strong!
We are not here to play, to dream, to drift;
We have hard work to do, and loads to lift;
Shun not the struggle—face it; 'tis God's gift.

Be strong!
Say not, "The days are evil. Who's to blame?"
And fold the hands and acquiesce—oh shame!
Stand up, speak out, and bravely, in God's name.

Be strong!
It matters not how deep entrenched the wrong,
How hard the battle goes, the day how long;
Faint not—fight on! Tomorrow comes the song.
> —MALTBIE DAVENPORT BABCOCK (1858-1901)[218]
> A Presbyterian minister His daughter collected his works and published them.

Oak trees are not grown in a day. It takes years for them to become, just as it takes time to become strong. To overcome a weakness is to bring strength to the weak one. Just as an oak tree is made over a period of years, if it ever comes time to cut the tree down, it is not done in one stroke but many well-planned hits.

Many strokes fell tall Oaks.
> —JOHN CLARKE (1596-1658)

Anyone can quit. That is the easy way out, but it takes guts to stick with something when it would be less painful to give up. This marks the difference between the weak and the strong.

The universal line of distinction between the strong and the weak is that one persists; the other hesitates, falters, trifles, and at last collapses or "caves in."

— EDWIN PERCY WHIPPLE (1819-1886)

American author, essayist, and critic

The sixteenth president of the United States, Abraham Lincoln, learned the lesson of not giving up. The chronology of his life is full of failures, disappointments, and challenges, as shown below:

1831	Failed in business
1832	Defeated for legislature
1833	Again failed in business
1834	Elected to legislature
1835	Sweetheart died
1836	Had nervous breakdown
1838	Defeated for speaker
1840	Defeated for elector
1843	Defeated for Congress
1846	Elected to Congress
1848	Defeated for Congress
1855	Defeated for Senate
1856	Defeated for Vice-President
1858	Defeated for Senate
1860	ELECTED PRESIDENT

The message is clear: Never Give Up! If the will is strong enough and a person is willing to keep on no matter what and to work hard, success shall come. The following poem says it well:

DON'T QUIT

When things go wrong, as they sometimes will,
When the road you're trudging seems all up hill,
When the funds are low and the debts are high,
And you want to smile, but you have to sigh,
When care is pressing you down a bit,
Rest, if you must — but don't you quit.

Life is queer with its twists and turns,
As everyone of us sometimes learns,
And many a failure turns about

When he might have won had he stuck it out;
Don't give up, though the pace seems slow —
You might succeed with another blow.

Often the goal is nearer than
It seems to a faint and faltering man,
Often the struggler has given up
When he might have captured the victor's cup.
And he learned too late, when the night slipped down,
How close he was to the golden crown.

Success is failure turned inside out —
The silver tint of the clouds of doubt —
And you never can tell how close you are,
It may be near when it seems afar;
So stick to the fight when you're hardest hit —
It's when things seem worst that you mustn't quit.
— AUTHOR UNKNOWN[219]

SUCCESS STORY:

ANDREW JACKSON

Andrew Jackson grew up among people who were ready to fight any time to defend their home. This led him into many fights. Any boy who dared to play a practical joke on Andrew found himself challenged to a battle. A schoolmate later recalled that Andrew would "never give up," even when another boy had him on the ground.

In 1780, British troops invaded the Southern Colonies. The thirteen-year-old Andrew and one of his brothers, Hugh, joined the mounted militia of South Carolina. In April 1781, a British raiding party captured Andrew and his other brother, Robert, who had also joined the militia. The British commander wanted his boots cleaned and ordered Andrew to scrub them. The boy refused, arguing that he had rights as a prisoner of war. The angry officer lashed out at Andrew with his sword, and the youth threw up his left hand to protect himself. The blade slashed Andrew's hand to the bone and cut him badly on the head. He carried scars from the wounds for the rest of his life.

During the war with Great Britain, the federal government commissioned Jackson a major general in the regular army. Jackson was assigned to command US forces along the southern coast. Before moving on to New Orleans, Jackson asked permission to seize Pensacola in Spanish Florida. The British had been using the town as a military base. Orders failed to arrive, so Jackson took the responsibility. He captured the town in a quick campaign. The victory left him free to supervise the defense of New Orleans.

Jackson arrived in the city on December 1, 1814, and found the people almost defenseless. Though ill with dysentery, he set a furious pace in preparing to defend the city. After several minor attacks, the British army of more than 8,000 men began its attack at dawn on January 8, 1815. The British marched up in close columns against earthworks defended by Jackson's artillery and riflemen. The attack ended in a terrible defeat for the British, who suffered 700 men killed, 1,400 wounded, and 500 captured. The American losses totaled only 7 men killed and 6 wounded. The victory made Jackson a national hero.

The same "never give up" attitude accompanied Jackson into the White House. The tall, lean Jackson stood straight as a soldier at the age of sixty-one. His bright blue eyes shone from a face wrinkled with age and illness. He had suffered tuberculosis and coughed almost all the time. He also had many severe headaches.

Jackson said in his inaugural address, "The Federal Constitution must be obeyed, state rights preserved, our national debt must be paid, direct taxes and loans avoided, and the Federal Union preserved. These are the objects I have in view, and regardless of all consequences will carry into effect."

SUCCESS NUGGETS:

Perseverance is a great element of success. If you only knock long enough and loud enough at the gate, you are sure to wake up somebody.
— HENRY WADSWORTH LONGFELLOW[220]

Courage and perseverance have a magical talisman, before which difficulties disappear and obstacles vanish into air.
— JOHN QUINCY ADAMS[221]

DON'T GIVE UP
'Twixt failure and success the point's so fine
Men sometimes know not when they touch the line,
Just when the pearl was waiting one more plunge,
How many a struggler has thrown in the sponge!
Then take this honey from the bitterest cup:
"There is no failure save in giving up!"[222]

EPILOGUE

The very substance of the ambitious is merely the shadow of a dream.
— SHAKESPEARE

Where there is no vision, the people perish.
— PROVERBS 29:18

The following three stories prove that nothing stops those with a dream:

1. HANS CHRISTIAN ANDERSEN (1805-1875):
    William T. Atwood shares the following about Hans Christian Andersen:

    Though it was probably not so intended, "The Ugly Duckling" is almost autobiographical of the author. Born in poverty and early orphaned, he was left to his own devices. Ungainly in person and of a dreamy disposition, his early youth was lonely and unhappy. His dreary hours were occupied in the construction of a puppet theater in which he produced the works of the great dramatists as well as his own efforts at play writing. But despite his apparent dullness, he was a keen observer of the people about him. His imagination saw through the obvious and endowed the homely affairs of life and the humdrum persons he met with the mystery and poetry that were later to make his fairy tales famous. Workaday citizens, touched by his wizardry, were to become kings and adventurers, the shopkeeper's daughter a princess; the storks on the chimney tops were to be transformed into fairy messengers; moles and field mice, larks and toads were to play parts in his stories; even the flax plant and the broken bottle were to tell their tales.

    Andersen's flair for dramatics led him to attempt successively to become an opera singer and a dancer. He failed in both, and in Copenhagen, where he had gone to study these

217

arts he was regarded as little better than a lunatic. However a few influential friends, and later the King, saw possibilities in the imaginative youth and befriended him. Presently he began to write. Various stories and romances appeared, and some were successful. Then came the Fairy Tales, which were an immediate success. The Ugly Duckling had become the Swan. Children and adults have from that day delighted in the many translations of his immortal book. Today a statue of Hans Christian Andersen, bought with pennies of school children, adorns a public square in Copenhagen.[223]

2.   AN UNKNOWN:

Harry Emerson Fosdick wrote the following:

Mr. Newton Baker, Secretary of War in President Wilson's cabinet, told me that after World War I he used to visit in the Federal hospitals the worst casualties of the American Army. One of the very worst was a man with both legs gone, one arm gone, both eyes gone, his face terribly mutilated, who was wheeled around the grounds of the hospital in a perambulator by a nurse, but who still was radiant and full of spirit. Nobody expected him to live. When later Mr. Baker met somebody from the hospital he said, "Did that young man live?" And the answer was, "Did he live? I'll say he did! He married his nurse!"

Marveling at the capacity of women to love, Mr. Baker put the matter by, until a few years later as trustee of Johns Hopkins University he received a letter from the president. They wished, said the president, to do an unusual thing, to hold a mid-semester convocation to bestow the degree of Doctor of Philosophy upon a young man who, though heavily handicapped, had done one of the most brilliant pieces of work ever done at the University. His name was that of the crippled veteran. Mr. Baker, quite incredulous that it could be the same man, but struck with that phrase, "heavily handicapped," made inquiries. Sure enough, it was he! Both legs gone, one arm gone, both eyes gone, but still, not part of the world's problem but part of the answer.

Not every handicapped person can win through to so conspicuous a result, but the spirit—the spirit that stays undefeated in spite of everything—is part of the solution, and those of us still strong and well who see it take another notch in our belts and go to our tasks again with fresh courage.[224]

3.   ENRICO CARUSO:

Dorothy Caruso shares the following account of the great tenor singer, Enrico Caruso, which demonstrates that nothing made him stop even in his older years of performance; he literally gave everything of himself:

Before the performance I went as usual to his dressing room and found him standing at the washstand, rinsing his throat. Suddenly I heard him say, "Look!" I looked and saw that the water in the basin was pink. "Darling, you brushed your teeth too hard," I said. He took another mouthful and spat it out. This time the water was red. Mario [his valet] said quietly, "I have the doctor's number." I said, "Tell him to bring adrenalin."

Enrico continued silently to wash his throat. Each time he said, "Look." At last he stopped. "Doro," he said, "Return to your place and no matter what happens do not move. The audience will be watching you, so be careful not to start a panic."

I obeyed, sick with fear, remembering that he had once said, "Tenors die sometimes on the stage after big note, from hemorrhage."

My seats were in the front row. The curtain rose a quarter of an hour late, and I knew that the doctor must have arrived . . . Enrico came running out . . .The audience applauded wildly. Standing close to the footlights, he began at once to sing. When he had finished he turned his back and reached for his handkerchief. I heard him give a little cough, but he came in on his cue, finished the phrase and turned away again. When he faced the audience I saw that the front of his smock was scarlet. A whisper blew through the house but stopped as he began to sing. This time it was an aria and he couldn't turn his back. From the wings Zirato's hand held out a towel. Enrico took it, wiped his lips and went on singing. Towel after towel was passed to him and still he sang on. All about him on the stage lay crimson towels. At last he finished the aria and ran off. The act was ended and the curtain came down.[225]

These three men were winners. They refused to give up because of handicaps, illness, or adverse circumstances. The comparison between a loser and a winner is captured in the following:

<u>Winner versus Loser</u>

1. A winner says, "Let's find out"; a loser says, "Nobody knows."

2. When a winner makes a mistake, he says, "I was wrong." When a loser makes a mistake, he says, "It wasn't my fault."

3. A winner goes through a problem; a loser goes around it and never gets past it.

4. A winner makes commitments; a loser makes promises.

5. A winner says, "I'm good but not as good as I ought to be." A loser says, "I'm not as bad as a lot of other people are."

6. A winner tries to learn from those who are superior to him. A loser tries to tear down those who are superior to him.

7. A winner says, "There ought to be a better way to do it." A loser says, "That's the way it's always been done here."

— AUTHOR UNKNOWN

BIBLIOGRAPHY

Arnault, M. A. & Panckoucke, C. L. F., *Life and Campaigns of Napoleon Bona-parte*, Boston, MA: Phillips, Sampson, & Co.: 1857.

Bennett, Arnold, *How to Live on 24 Hours a Day*, Hyattsville, MD: Shambling Gate Press: 2000.

Carnegie, Dale, *How to Stop Worrying and Start Living*, New York, NY: Simon & Schuster: 1948.

Carnegie, Dale, *How to Win Friends and Influence People*, New York, NY: Simon and Schuster: 1948.

Caruso, Dorothy, *Enrico Caruso*, New York, NY: Simon & Schuster: 1945.

Debre, Patrice, *Louis Pasteur*, Baltimore, MD: John Hopkins University Press: 1994.

Dolan, Edward F. Dolan, Jr., *Pasteur and the Invisible Giants*, New York, NY: Dodd, Mead & Co.: 1958.

Geison, Gerald L., *The Private Science of Louis Pasteur*, Princeton, NJ: Princeton University: 1995.

Guest, Edgar A. Guest, *Collected Verse of Edgar A. Guest*, Chicago, IL: The Reilly & Lee Co.: 1934.

Hacker, Louis M., *The World of Andrew Carnegie*, New York, NY: J. B. Lippincott Co.: 1968.

Hawkins, Hugh, ed., *Booker T. Washington and His Critics*, Lexington, MA: D.C. Heath & Co.: 1974.

Hedrick, Joan D., *Harriet Beecher Stowe: A Life*, New York: Oxford University Press: 1994.

Hutchinson, William T., *Cyrus Hall McCormack*, New York, NY: The Century Co.: 1930.

Keller, Helen, *The Story of My Life*, Garden City, NY: Doubleday & Co.: 1902.

Long, Gavin, *MacArthur as Military Commander*, Portman Square, London: B. T. Batsford Ltd.: 1969.

Marlow, Joan, *The Great Women*, New York, NY: Galahad Books: 1979.

Petry, Ann, *Harriet Tubman: Conductor on the Underground Railroad*, New York: HarperCollins Publishers: 1955.

Smith, Jessie Carney, ed., *Notable Black American Women*, Detroit, MI: Gale Research: 1992.

INDEX

Clark, Adam 186

Clark, John 212

Cicero 142

Coleridge, Samuel Taylor 158

Collier, Jeremy 133

Coolidge, Calvin 87, 210

Cronin, A. J. 70

Dempsey, Jack 105

DeMontaigne, Michel 52

De Paul, Vincent 39

De Saint-Exupery 124

deSalas, Francis 75

deSeversky, Alexander 127-128

Dickens, Charles 152

Disralli, Benjamin 61, 98, 177, 194, 197

Dossey, Larry, M.D. 114-115

Douglas, Lloyd C. 86, 143

Douglas, Stephen A. 139

Downs, Hugh 3

Dronais 126

Dulles, John Foster 176

Dutton, Dean C. 121, 166

Edison, Thomas A. 42, 68-69, 96-98, 139
142, 144, 182

Edwards, Tyrone 109

Ehrlich, Paul 31-32

Einstein, Albert 144

Eisenhower, Dwight D. 121, 143, 177

Emerson, Ralph Waldo 6, 61, 77, 96, 101,
133, 159, 164, 171, 179, 182

Epicurus 140

Farrow, William G. 144

Field, Cyrus W. 185

Forbes, B.C. 140

Ford, Henry 62, 105, 136, 204

Fosdick, Harry Emerson 138, 179, 218

Foster, Willa A. 149

Franklin, Benjamin 67, 115, 144, 200, 204

Fromm, Erich 4

Frost, Robert 127

Froude, James Anthony 164

Fuller, Thomas 4,

Garrison, William Lloyd 91

Gasset, Jose O. 183

George, David Lloyd 142

Gibran, Kahlil 57

Glasgow, Ellen 167

Goldsmith, Oliver 139, 156

Griswold, Alfred Whitney 4

Guest, Edgar A. 102-103, 170

Hale, Edward Everett 88

Hammarskjold, Dag 141

Harriman, Edward H. 85-86

Hazlitt, William 46

Heschel, Abraham J. 4

Holmes, Oliver Wendell 171

Holmes, Sr., Oliver Wendell 127

Hood, Paxton 45

Hooker, Richard 5

Howell, James 20

Hubbard, Elbert 21, 192

Hubbard, Kin 29, 40

Index

NOTES

[1] Dutton, Dean C., *Quests and Conquests* (Life Service Publishing Co., Guthrie, OK: 1933), p. 18.

[2] *Ibid.*, p. 179.

[3] Howell, Clinton T., *Lines to Live By* (Thomas Nelson Inc., Nashville, TN: 1972), p. 155.

[4] Tan, Paul Lee, ThD, *Encyclopedia of 7,700 Illustrations,* (Assurance Publishers, Rockville, Maryland: 1979), #4038.

[5] Tan, #4033.

[6] Frank, Leonard Roy, ed, *Quotationary* (Random House, New York, NY: 1999), p.59.

[7] *Ibid.*, p. 232.

[8] *Ibid.*, p. 157.

[9] Howell, p. 156.

[10] Watson, Lillian E., *Light from Many Lamps* (Simon and Schuster, New York, NY: 1951), p. 133.

[11] Debre, Patrice, *Louis Pasteur* (Johns Hopkins University Press: Baltimore, MD: 1994), p. 449.

[12] Tan, #2034.

[13] Hacker, Louis M., *The World of Andrew Carnegie* (J. B. Lippincott Co., New York, NY:1968), p. 358.

[14] Dutton, p. 49.

[15] Petry, Ann, *Harriet Tubman: Conductor on the Underground Railroad* (HarperCollins Publishers, New York, NY: 1955), p. 94.

[16] *Ibid.*, p. 101.

[17] Watson, p. 159.

[18] Howell, p. 63.

[19] *Ibid.*, p. 63.

[20] Dutton, p. 174.

[21] Frank, p. 194.

[22] Keller, Helen, *The Story of My Life* (Doubleday & Co., Garden City, NY: 1902), pp. 334-335.

[23] Frank, p. 206.

[24] Dutton, p. 18.

[25] Tan, #3522.

[26] Frank, p. 265.

[27] Dutton, p. 172.

[28] Howell, p. 180.

[29] Frank, p. 265.

30   *Ibid.*, p. 157.
31   *Ibid.*, p. 188.
32   Dutton, p. 8.
33   Carnegie, Dale, *How to Stop Worrying and Start Living* (Simon & Schuster: New York, NY: 1948), p. 172.
34   Dutton, p. 108.
35   Frank, p. 435.
36   *Ibid.*, p. 173.
37   Carnegie, *How to Stop Worrying*, p. 173.
38   Dutton, p. 15.
39   Watson, p. 92.
40   *Ibid.*, p.93.
41   *Ibid.*, p.29.
42   Howell, p. 87.
43   Watson, p. 55.
44   Bettger, Frank, *How I Raised Myself from Failure to Success in Selling* (Prentice- Hall, Inc., Englewood Cliffs, NJ: 1949), p. 116.
45   *Ibid.*, p. 257.
46   Tan, #6084.
47   Howell, p. 42.
48   Bettger, p. 165.
49   *Ibid.*
50   Tan, #6369
51   *Ibid.*, #6376
52   Watson, p. 152.
53   *Ibid.*, p. 183.
54   Howell, p. 186.
55   Frank, p. 159.
56   Watson, p. 179.
57   *Ibid.*
58   Dutton, p. 23.
59   Watson, p. xiii.
60   Tan, #1633.
61   Tan, #4095.
62   *Ibid.*, #3637.
63   *Ibid.*, #7701.
64   Hutchinson, William T., *Cyrus Hall McCormick* (The Century Co., New York, NY: 1930), p. 293.
64   *Ibid.*
66   Watson, p. 131.
67   *Ibid.*, p. 130.
68   Howell, p. 185.
69   Frank, p. 382.
70   Tan, #1159.
71   Keller, pp. 53, 70.

Notes

72 Howell, p. 158.
73 Watson, p. 30.
74 Tan, #4279.
75 Dutton, p. 17.
76 Howell, p. 117.
77 Frank, p. 311.
78 Howell, p. 110.
79 Bettger, p. 207.
80 Frank, p. 256.
81 Tan, #1633.
82 Felleman, Hazel, *Best Loved Poems of the American People* (Garden City Books, Garden City, NY: 1936), p. 91.
83 Dutton, p. 15.
84 Howell, p. 43.
85 Watson, p. 183.
86 Dutton, p. 13.
87 Carnegie, *How to Stop Worrying*, p. 153.
88 *Ibid.*, p. 154.
89 *Ibid.*, p. 161.
90 Tan, #4527.
91 *Ibid.*, #4524.
92 Frank, p. 319.
93 Tan, #4525.
94 Dutton, p. 47.
95 *Ibid.*, #419.
96 *Ibid.*, p. 256.
97 Arnault, M. A., and C. L. F. Panckoucke, *Life and Campaigns of Napoleon Bonaparte* (Phillips, Sampson, & Co., Boston, MA: 1857). p. 9.
98 Dutton, p. 19.
99 Keller, p. 309.
100 Dutton, p. 109.
101 Howell, p. 23.
102 *Ibid.*, p. 25.
103 Dutton, p. 28.
104 *Ibid.*, p. 298.
105 *Ibid.*, p. 77.
106 Carrell, Alexis, MD, *Reader's Digest* (Pleasantville, NY: Reader's Digest Assn., 1941), pp. 34-35
107 Tan, #4571.
108 Dossey, Larry, MD, *Healing Words: The Power of Prayer and the Practice of Medicine* (San Francisco, CA: HarperCollins Publishers: 1993).
109 Johnson, Joseph S., *A Field of Diamonds* (Broadman Press, Nashville, TN: 1974), p. 153
110 Tan, #4550.
111 *Ibid.*, p. 152.

112 *Ibid.*, #4569.
113 *Ibid.*, #4605.
114 *Ibid.*, #1875, #4511.
115 *Ibid.*, #4583.
116 *Ibid.*, #4574.
117 *Ibid.*, #1510.
118 *Guideposts*, May 1982.
119 Dutton, p. 77.
120 Tan, #1856.
121 Dutton, p. 27.
122 Tan, #4567.
123 Felleman, p. 326.
124 Debre, p. 482.
125 Frank, p. 583.
126 Watson, p. 94.
127 Felleman, pp. 109-110.
128 Carnegie, Dale, *How to Win Friends and Influence People* (Simon and Schuster, New York, NY: 1948), pp. 6-10.
129 Howell, p. 158.
130 *Ibid.*, p. 23.
131 *Ibid.*, p. 63.
132 *Ibid.*, p. 187.
133 Keller, p. 305.
134 Watson, p. 155.
135 Dutton, p. 181.
136 Tan, #3516.
137 Howell, p. 95.
138 Dutton, p. 16.
139 Tan, #2845.
140 Dutton, p. 181.
141 Frank, p. 156.
142 Dutton, p.180.
143 *Ibid.*, p. 200.
144 Howell, p. 183.
145 Felleman, p. 122.
146 *Ibid.*, pp. 129-130.
147 Howell, p. 162.
148 Debre, p. 493.
149 Felleman, pp. 88-89.
150 Dutton, p. 115.
151 *Ibid.*, p. 19.
152 *Ibid.*, p. 79.
153 *Ibid.*, p.12.
154 Frank, p. 405.
155 Howell, p. 158.

Notes

156 Dutton, p. 181.
157 Carnegie, *How to Stop Worrying,* p. 178.
158 Dutton, p. 64.
159 Howell, p. 30.
160 Tan, #5801.
161 *Ibid.*, #4139.
162 Dutton, p. 23.
163 *Ibid.*, p. 134.
164 *Ibid.*, p. 101.
165 Watson, p. 166.
166 Dutton, p. 114.
167 *Ibid.*, p. 174.
168 *Ibid.*, p. 336.
169 Howell, p. 183.
170 Bettger, pp. 5, 7.
171 *Ibid.*, p. 7.
172 *Ibid.*, p. 10.
173 Howell, p. 186.
174 Dutton, p. 114.
175 Hacker, p. 355.
176 Frank, p. 833.
177 *Ibid.*, p. 204.
178 *Ibid.*
179 Carnegie, *How to Stop Worrying,* p. 2.
180 Dutton, p. 33.
181 Howell, p. 29.
182 Tan, #4334.
183 Caruso, Dorothy, *Enrico Caruso His Life and Death* (Simon and Schuster, New York, NY: 1945), p. 146.
184 *Ibid.*, p. 85.
185 *Ibid.*, p. 259.
186 Tan, #3865.
187 Dutton, p. 111.
188 *Ibid.*, p. 37.
189 *Ibid.*, p. 29.
190 Howell, p. 28.
191 Bettger, p. 30.
192 *Ibid.*, p. 32.
193 Fellemen, p. 143.
194 Watson, p. 152.
195 Alexander, A. L., *Poems that Touch the Heart* (Doubleday, New York, NY: 1941), pp.2-3
196 Long, Gavin, *MacArthur as Military Commander* (B. T. Batsford Ltd., Portman Square, London: 1969), p. 224.
197 *Ibid.*, p. 79.

[198] Watson, p. 38.
[199] Howell, p. 30.
[200] Dutton, p. 226.
[201] Tan, #2956.
[202] Frank, p. 156.
[203] Dutton, p. 105.
[204] Caruso, *Enrico Caruso: His Life and Death,* p. 144.
[205] Dutton, p. 41.
[206] Carnegie, Dale,
[207] Dutton, p. 47.
[208] *Ibid.,* p. 58.
[209] *Ibid.,* p. 119.
[210] *Ibid.,* p. 27.
[211] Howell, p. 36.
[212] Watson, p. 103.
[213] Tan, #4394
[214] Watson, p. 152.
[215] Howell, p. 35.
[216] Bettger, p. 206.
[217] Howell, p. 95.
[218] *Ibid.,* p. 34.
[219] Felleman, pp. 113-114.
[220] Watson, p. 141.
[221] *Ibid.,* p. 141.
[222] Howell, p. 86.
[223] Andersen, Hans Christian, *Andersen's Fairy Tales* (The John C. Winston Co., Philadelphia, PA: 1926
[224] Watson, pp. 93-94.
[225] Caruso, pp. 237-238.